SOUL MATES

A COLLECTION OF TRUE LOVE STORIES

DEBORAH FAY

Soul Mates: A Collection of True Love Stories

© Disruptive Publishing 2024

Published by Disruptive Publishing

17 Spencer Avenue

Deception Bay QLD 4508

Australia

www.disruptivepublishing.com.au

All Rights Reserved. No part of this publication may be reproduced, distributed or transmitted in any form, or by any means, including photocopying, recording, or any other electronic methods, without the prior written permission of the author or publisher. Brief quotations that are credited to the publication and the author are permitted.

Each of the contributing authors in this book retain the rights to their individual contributions, all of which have been printed as a part of this compilation with their permission. Each author is responsible for any opinions expressed within their own stories.

ISBN 978-1-7637283-5-6 Print

ISBN 978-1-7637283-4-9 Ebook

INTRODUCTION

Something I learned quickly when I moved into the publishing space was that readers want to be moved. They might not be aware that they do, but it is true.

They are looking for experiences that will either lift them up and take them to places within themselves that they haven't been before, or they are seeking opportunities to feel things they don't normally experience in their day to day lives.

So what is it about *love* stories that captures us so completely? Is it the thrill of discovering the moments when two lives intertwine and then watching that unfold into excruciatingly beautiful and unpredictable experiences that neither could have imagined?

Or is it the reminder we seek that love—no matter how simple or complex—because it has the power to transcend every boundary and every hardship.

INTRODUCTION

In an uncertain world, true love stories remind us of the fact that magic still exists, and that maybe, one day, we might stumble into a chance meeting, a meaningful glance, or a single word that changes everything our lives and lifts us up in a way that only love can do.

In this book, Soul Mates, you'll find a collection of real-life love stories, each as unique as the people who shared them. Some have loved and lost, only to find love once again in the unlikeliest of places. Others have walked through life with a partner by their side, facing life's joys and trials with steady devotion. And some found their match in fleeting encounters, proving that even brief connections can leave lasting marks on our hearts. These are not fairy tales, but stories grounded in the messy, beautiful reality of each of the author's lives.

We live in a world that often romanticises love in the grandest of gestures, from sweeping serenades to love-at-first-sight moments. But true love, as many of these stories show, reveals itself in so many more ways—from a knowing glance shared across a room, the squeeze of a hand during a difficult time, or the simple joy of everyday companionship.

Each page in this book is a testament to love's endurance, its unexpected twists, and the way it shapes us in ways we may never have imagined.

What you hold in your hands is more than a book; it's an invitation. It's an invitation to walk alongside each of the authors as they open their hearts and share their stories.

Each one of them have risked heartbreak and loved fear-

INTRODUCTION

lessly because they each believed in love's ability to heal and transform.

In reading their experiences, you may find glimpses of your own story, or perhaps, a glimmer of hope for what's yet to come.

As you turn each page, may you feel a spark of connection to the universal force that binds us all. Because whether we love once in a lifetime or a thousand times over, each love leaves its mark on our hearts.

Soul Mates: A Collection of True Love Stories is a patchwork of unforgettable moments that will stay with us long after you've finished reading the book.

So, dear reader, as you dive into the lives of our beautiful authors and hear about their journeys of real love, may you find yourself uplifted, moved, and inspired to recognise the beauty of love in all its many forms in your own life.

Whether you are in the midst of your own love story or waiting for the first chapter to begin, remember: the stories within these pages are proof that love is out there, waiting for each of us and it will find us in its own time, in its own way.

Welcome to the timeless journey of love, and may these stories remind you that we are never truly alone on this path.

Yours in magic,
    Deborah

INTRODUCTION

Deborah Fay is the Founder and CEO of Disruptive Publishing. If you would like to know more about becoming a published author, you can go to www.disruptivepublishing.com.au or you can reach out to Deb via her direct email: deb@disruptivepublishing.com.au. She would love to hear from you.

1
PITY ABOUT THE MULLET
ALBINA PORRACIN

SOUL MATES

ANTHONY and I first met each other as children, and I remember him being the quiet one, watching as I played with his cousins Maria, Carmel, and Mathew at family get-togethers and weddings.

His grandmother and my grandparents were from the same town in Sicily, Mascali. His grandparents' farm on Mount Etna was destroyed by lava from a volcanic eruption, forcing them to move to Annunziata, then to Giarre, and then to Mascali on Via Umberto (Umberto Street) where Anthony's late Mum was raised. Anyway, moving to Mascali made his grandparents and my grandparents Pisani (people who are from the same village or town). Anthony's grandfather died before he was born, and his father died when he was eighteen months old, so his mother and grandmother raised him together. Anthony's aunt was married to my great-uncle (and I know what you're thinking, no we are not related!).

I was very close to my grandparents, and when my Nonno was older and it was harder for him to drive longer distances, I would drive him and my Nanna whenever they needed me to. Looking back, I feel they wanted me to meet Anthony. There was one time I drove them out to Green Valley, where Anthony lived, a good hour away from Eastwood, where we lived. We went to see Anthony's grandmother, a usually very active woman in her nineties, who was recovering from severe pneumonia.

I was about seventeen or eighteen years old at this time. I remember my hair being a lot thicker back then, hair that was long and curly that I had pulled back in a low ponytail, I wore big hoop earrings, a white long-sleeved shirt, and my favourite blue jeans. I drove a Nissan Pulsar Sport with no air-conditioning. I remember that my future mother-in-law had air-conditioning in her home, and she was showing it to my grandparents because we didn't have air-conditioning. They may have needed it more out their way—it was cooler in Eastwood.

I sat with my grandparents and met Anthony's dog, Blacky. And I met Anthony again—he was really nice, and easy to talk to. He wore a flannelette shirt and black trackies, and he had a mullet that fell into ringlets of hair at the back. He played with the furthest curl of his mullet without stopping conversation or breaking eye contact. He sometimes twists his much shorter fringe the same way now as if it still had the same length, and I have a little giggle because it reminds me of back then. I don't think he realised he did it; he just did it subconsciously. I remember thinking, *'He's nice, but pity about the mullet.'*

We didn't see each other for a while after that. Then, in 1994, it was my grandparents' fiftieth wedding anniversary. They decided to renew their vows and have a big reception at what used to be an Italian reception venue called the Mediterranean House and La Mirage Function Centre, at Five Dock.

I remember wearing a slim, emerald-green dress; it had a halter-neck with a diamante at the front of the neckline at the beginning of the halter and a split in the front of the skirt. My grandparents wanted me to speak in Italian at their reception—waiting to ride a rollercoaster would've made me less nervous than doing that, and I'm not the biggest fan of heights! Fortunately, a cousin from Melbourne, who was staying with us, helped me check over my speech.

As I was getting ready that afternoon, a voice in my head said, *'You are going to meet someone special tonight.'* I thought, 'If I do, I do.' I didn't pay much attention to it. I was twenty years old, and marriage was closer to the last thing I wanted to do then. I would tell everyone I was too independent, and I wasn't looking!

At the reception I was sitting at one of the tables with my siblings and cousins. Anthony was at the table behind me. I didn't really notice much—or maybe I did, he was in a suit, and I liked a man in a suit back then. I remembered him from our last meeting, and I definitely noticed he no longer had that mullet! He came over to my table and leaned over to make me notice him as he talked to his cousin. I said to my cousin, Frank, "Check out this guy!" I laughed and I said, "Hi" to start the conversation. "I remember you! I came to your house, and you have a dog named Blacky," I continued. We talked briefly, he was very friendly, and I could see he was nice, and he had happy eyes which showed me his beautiful soul. But I was also conscious of my very strict dad and what he would do if he saw us talking.

Anthony says his first impression of me was when he noticed me while talking to his cousin Maria, who is like a sister to him. She was also at my grandparents' fiftieth wedding anniversary. In his words, he thought I was 'hot'.

I told my parents straight out that I was going out on a date with Anthony. I didn't think about it much, I just did it. I was expecting my dad to flip his lid as usual, but I didn't care. Anthony asked me—not my dad—if he could take me out. I hated that old-fashioned idea of asking my father for permission. It was like we were still living in the old days where people would ask my dad instead of me. It was embarrassing. I always thought I would go out with the person who asked me, not the one who asked my father. Anthony was respectful and kind, and he respected me first.

Anthony asked me to the movies, and although he suggested an action movie, he let me choose and I picked *Priscilla, Queen of the Desert*. Afterwards, we went to a café. I was nervous and got an upset stomach, but it passed! It was hilarious; I was anxious to impress him, but we got along well. I drove us to the Roxy Picture Theatre, the one from my childhood. Anthony had driven an hour to meet me, so I drove us to Parramatta and back, as he had another hour's drive home.

When we started dating, my intuition told me he was *the one* straight away. I had a 'gut' feeling about it and a feeling in my heart too. We dated, it was all so easy and then we got engaged. We discussed what our future life would be like. We agreed that when we were married, we would be partners. We've always supported each other. One picks up when the other is ill or busy. We are independent people who choose to be together and love each other. I am independent, and Anthony is independent, but we help each other and support each other. We make sure to spend time together, but we also have our own activities, for instance, I have writing, art and meditation; he has soccer and sport.

When did I think we were soul mates? Straight away. We always have a choice, but I *knew*. I wanted to be sure, so we were engaged three months after we met and married eighteen months after that. We talked about being partners in our marriage and agreed that if we both worked full-time, we would share the housework. I would cook, and he would clean up. It was important to me to make sure this would happen because I saw a very unfair division of home duties growing up.

What I admire most about Anthony is that he loves me. He is kind, calm, funny, and serious when he needs to be. He is gentle towards me, caring, and protective, but he also supports my adventures, my self-growth, and my health. He encourages my writing, coaching, and healing. He says, "Do it," and tells me how proud he is of me. I'm grateful for that, and I will be forever. However, we both have our stubborn streaks: he's a Leo and I'm a Scorpio.

Communication and trust have always been the foundation of our relationship. We make it a priority to be open with each other, whether it's about our feelings, challenges, or even small decisions. Over the years, we've learned that effective communication is key to resolving issues and moving forward. Even when we don't agree, we make an effort to listen and understand each other's point of view. Trust has never been questioned between us, and that's something I'm grateful for. We've built a relationship where we trust each other to make decisions in the best interest of our family, and we feel secure in knowing we have each other's backs, no matter what.

Over the years, we've grown—not just as individuals—but as a couple. When we first got together, we were young and still figuring out who we were. But as time passed, we've been able to grow into the people we are today because we supported each other's journeys. I've seen Anthony grow as a father, husband, and individual, and he's been by my side as I've pursued new ventures. Our growth has always been intertwined because we make an effort to nurture each other's goals and dreams. We've learned to evolve together rather than apart, and that has been key to sustaining our relationship for over twenty-seven years.

There have been so many memorable experiences throughout our marriage, but one that stands out is the day we bought our house by the beach. It was a dream for both of us, a place where we could escape the busyness of life, relax, and spend time as a couple and with our kids. I remember walking along the beach that first evening, feeling like we had achieved something special together. It wasn't just about the house; it was about the journey we had taken to get there, the sacrifices and hard work, and the realisation that we were building a life full of love and adventure. Every time we go to the beach house now, it brings back those feelings of joy and accomplishment.

The best advice I could give to couples about maintaining a strong relationship is to always communicate and never take each other for granted. Relationships aren't perfect, and there will be challenges, but being open and honest with each other is key. Show appreciation for the little things, support each other's dreams, and always make time for each other. Even after twenty-seven years, we still go on 'dates', have our special moments, and make sure we're growing together. Be patient, be kind, and most importantly, never forget *why* you fell in love in the first place. Life gets busy, but a strong relationship will always thrive when you nurture it, even through the ups-and-downs.

We connect through our shared values, frequent conversations, walks together and, of course, our family. Marcus, our oldest son, once said, "Mum likes to cook, and Dad likes to eat,"

—a simple but fitting example of our dynamic. We've built our little empire together, creating investments, and enjoy spending time walking along the beach when we visit the beach house. We watch movies and TV shows together and share our home and life with family and friends.

One of our most memorable moments was getting married. Reflecting on it, we both found the experience joyful, even with a quirky priest! Father Eugene had an unusual way of officiating. Interestingly, Anthony's father was also named Eugene, so we saw this as a positive sign, despite the priest's eccentricity. We both hold the reading from Corinthians 13:4 close to our hearts, as it continues to resonate deeply with us:

'Love is patient and kind. It is never jealous, boastful, or conceited. It is not rude or self-seeking. It is not easily angered and keeps no record of wrongs. Love does not delight in evil but rejoices with the truth. It always protects, always trusts, always hopes, and always perseveres. Love never fails.'

This reading has shaped our understanding of love as something that requires patience and kindness, not possession. We work on our relationship daily, knowing that it's a choice we both continue to make.

We spent our first anniversary on the bridge in the Chinese garden at the Nurragingy Reserve, at Doonside. It was just the two of us, renewing our vows by the lake. We took a booklet from our wedding the year before and looked through it together. The moment was peaceful, beautiful, and romantic, marking a special time for just the two of us.

Other milestones include the birth of our three children.

Seeing them for the first time, watching them grow, and then witnessing *their* milestones is incredibly fulfilling.

One of the hardest times for us was when Anthony's mother was dying of cancer. She spent her final days in our home, surrounded by love. I was pregnant with our second son, Thomas. During this time, and while Anthony was grieving, he was made redundant. Financial strain from my leave-from-work and his redundancy added pressure, but we saw the situation as an opportunity for him to care for his mother, which felt perfect in its own way. With community nurses' help, Anthony looked after her, and I did what I could despite showing early signs of a condition called Eosinophilic esophagitis (EoE for short) and managing my pregnancy.

Another significant challenge came when I was undergoing allergy testing for EoE and lost a baby I was carrying at four months. After already enduring family deaths and past trauma, the loss broke me. I stopped eating, and my health deteriorated to the point where the doctor threatened hospitalisation. With Anthony's unwavering support and my sister's help, I gradually recovered.

After this, we ran early childhood services for nine years before deciding I needed more time with our children. We sold the centres, and I transitioned into studying Reiki, ThetaHealing®, and Psychology, and started my energy healing business, as well as my Business and Finance Mentoring and Coaching Business Anthony went back to work part-time, running his bookkeeping business while helping to manage our rental properties.

During the COVID pandemic our daughter, Selina, faced serious health issues, including sports-induced hyponatremia and ulcerative colitis (UC). She experienced brain swelling, and there were moments when we didn't know if she'd make it through the night but thank God she did. With research and collaboration with her medical team, we got her into remission. Anthony and I supported, Selina, our boys and each other, and it strengthened our bond even further.

As we've grown older, so has our relationship. Our love has deepened into something confident and unwavering. We share the same values of love, loyalty, family and support, never experiencing jealousy or unkindness. While we have moments of teasing, we always know it comes from a place of love.

Anthony has always influenced me positively, offering support and encouragement in everything I do. Whether it's offering advice or simply listening, his love has helped me grow into a better person. He is proud of me writing books, and going on to do things many others won't, like recently appearing on a TV show.

We keep the romance alive by prioritising time for each other. We spend quality time together, and ensure we express our love even when life gets busy. Hugs, "*I love you*"s, and thoughtful gestures are small but meaningful ways we stay connected.

Communication is key for us. Whether it's talking in person, sending love notes or texts throughout the day, we stay connected and let each other know we're always there.

Our dreams are simple, yet meaningful: to be happy

together for as long as possible, to stay healthy, to continue to be financially secure, travel, and see the world. We want to leave a legacy for our children and eventually move down to the coast to live by the water permanently.

We see ourselves healthy and happy, with our children and their families around us. Grandchildren will be part of our lives, and our bond will remain strong. We hope to continue spending special days together as a family. More time at the beach, enjoying life, and having fun together will be a key focus for us. Celebrating special days together, keeping our relationship strong, and our relationship with our children strong as well.

To me, a soul mate is someone who loves you unconditionally, respects you, and always puts your needs before others. It's a deep connection of love and understanding. We nurture our connection through constant communication, physical touch, and care. We talk, listen, and make sure we're always there for each other.

Anthony and I have shared many spiritual moments together, from the birth of our children to supporting each other through life's challenges. We say the rosary together and light candles for others, and these moments of prayer strengthen our bond.

Early in our relationship there was some family pressure and outside opinions, but we quickly learned to trust our instincts and make decisions based on what was best for us.

Anthony is always supportive of my dreams, helping me turn them into reality. He's never jealous, only proud, and encourages me to pursue whatever I set my heart on. I do the same for him, by supporting his dreams.

My advice to others is that I think you need to love yourself first. You need to be independent and happy with who you are before finding someone else. Don't look for a partner out of desperation or a sense of incompleteness and the need to make yourself feel better. When you're confident in yourself, your soul mate will appear when you least expect it.

I'm most grateful for the trust we have in each other. Knowing that we are loyal and love each other is a blessing. We have support for each other, and we both carry a little extra when the other needs it. For example, I have had four surgical procedures over the last few months and Anthony has stepped up and been there for me and has taken on more of my responsibilities with our youngest while I recovered. He has been patient and understanding, and he wanted to be there for me. He attended medical appointments with me each time, waited with me before I went into surgery, and was there to pick me up afterwards. It's a blessing.

We stay committed as soul mates by putting our first, taking things one day at a time, and stepping up to support each other whenever needed. We balance things out and make sure our relationship remains strong despite any challenges.

Albina Porracin is a dedicated wealth strategist, coach, author, intuitive and founder of The Academy of Life and Money. With expertise in mindfulness, financial literacy, and personal development, she empowers individuals—particularly women—to master their mindset and create financial independence and heal blocks. Through her courses, books, and coaching, Albina helps clients build thriving businesses, achieve life balance, and manifest their dreams, making a positive impact on their financial and personal lives.

2

TWIN FLAMES

AMANDA GILL

I MET my twin flame for the first time in real life in the baggage claim of Hobart Airport. Standing in that brightly lit open space I waited, surrounded by travellers arriving in Tasmania. People coming home, people arriving on business, people coming to explore this beautiful part of the world I am lucky enough to call my home.

As I stood there, somehow nervous and calm at the same time, I let the noise of the airport wash over me: the comings and goings of busy travellers, the laughter and exclamations of love and joy that is shared at happy airport reunions, the bing-bong of the overhead speakers calling for lost passengers to make their way to the departure lounge, the sound of coffee being made in the café, the tsk-tsk of the milk-frother, the grind and clank of the bag carousel making its endless loops on squeaky tracks as it deposits its loads of suitcases, parcels, and bags to the patiently awaiting owners.

As a traveller myself, having spent many hours of my life in what seems like thousands of different arrival halls, standing there surrounded by the essence of airport life I felt safe and comforted as I waited for this next big adventure in my life to begin.

I had never heard the term 'Twin Flame' before I met Joshua, never knew what it meant or that a higher connection of souls was even a possibility.

Of course, I had heard of and knew what a soul mate was.

Does a soulmate have to be a lover, do you think? Someone only with whom you have an intimate relationship? Or can it be someone you have a close bond with? Your best friend? Your close relative? Someone who just 'gets' you and you them? Perhaps even a beloved pet?

Can you have more than one soul mate in a lifetime? I

certainly think so. I have even met a few people who were important enough in my life to qualify as a mate to my soul.

A clairvoyant once told me that my Grandma, who passed away when I was small, was my soulmate; that we had spent many past lives together, always finding each other, in different forms, as our souls were inexplicably drawn together.

Twin flames are believed to differ from a soul mate in that it only occurs when one soul is actually split into two and then sent to two different bodies. To live out their lives separately until, hopefully, they are lucky enough to find each other amongst the billions of people who live on this planet. Often described as intense soul connections or 'Mirror' souls because being around your twin flame can mirror back to you your deepest fears, insecurities and challenges.

On the flip side, however, your twin flame can also bring about the most powerful healing as you work together to overcome these insecurities. They challenge us to do better and be better as together we move closer and closer to a more conscious relationship that is intense and powerful, rare and strong.

My twin flame and I had actually met almost three months earlier, as many do in this modern Internet-driven world, online. Both of us swiping right and somehow finding each other amongst the chaos that online dating can be.

Imagine a woman in her early forties trying to find herself and her purpose in life. Fresh from a divorce that was just like the marriage that had come before it: amicable but passionless, friendly but beige.

Imagine her life falling apart, moving out of her home, quitting her job, everything changing and spinning; not out of control exactly, but away from all that she had known and that had felt familiar for so long. Not yet able to see what the universe had in store for her, but hoping and trusting that it would be okay.

Now, imagine a man onboard a ship out on the crystal blue waters of the Timor Sea. Working hard with chains and anchors and the elements. Imagine he too is fresh from a separation, but this one, toxic in its nature, left him fighting to find himself in the wreckage that was left of his life. Believing that he was unworthy. Believing that he was un-empathetic. Believing he was undeserving of love.

Now imagine them on opposite sides of the country, both making those tentative steps to reach out to others, putting themselves out there in the online dating world and seeing what happened.

Were they ready to do this to themselves? No, they weren't! Or should I say *WE* weren't because this is *our* story. Our story of not being ready but doing it anyway. Our story of finally coming home. Coming home to yourself, finding meaning in life again, recognising our flames in each other and finally coming home to each other.

Finally understanding that everything that had come before, everything that we had thought love looked like, everything we had been taught by others to expect, was NOT anything like how it was about to be for us.

From that first electronic message that was sent across the airwaves we were drawn together as only twin flames can be, and before we knew it our lives were lovingly entangled and entwined in ways that neither of us had ever known before.

And so we connected immediately. Those first conversations already showing our similarities, and we quickly made plans to meet in real life.

This Seafarer works away from our beautiful home state of Tasmania and was due to return a few days before Christmas. But the universe, in its wisdom, had other plans for us.

Maybe it knew that these particular twin flames, after waiting so long to find one another, needed time to really get to know each other before actually meeting.

Maybe it knew that slowing things down was exactly what we both needed to fully open up to not only the possibility of love but also the possibility of our intense twin flame reunion.

It was the ending of the time the world knows as COVID. Things were starting to pick back up again, the world starting to move forward through this scary pandemic, but only just so.

Australia's states were slowly opening their borders to each other, but unfortunately the one Josh worked in was still firmly closed.

Previous 'bubbles' that had existed were no longer in effect and feared that if the crew who lived out-of-state left to go home during their five-week leave they wouldn't be able to return to this state for the next crew-change. The company that Josh works for asked that he and his fellow out-of-staters stay close by, in that state, so as to return to work at the beginning of their next swing freely and unencumbered by the ever-changing rules and policies that were still happening and which couldn't be predicted from state to state at the time.

With that decision our first meeting was put on hold for at least ten weeks.

Ten weeks!

Ten full weeks before he could even think of returning home. Ten weeks before we could be in the same space together.

Even though it was still very early on neither of us could bear the thought of our conversations stopping. So it was an easy yes to the question of, "Do we keep chatting or not?" Both of us wanting very much to keep getting to know each other.

We agreed that if anything changed for either of us, we would be honest and open about it, no harm done, no expectations or promises. Both of us acknowledging and understanding that clear communication was extremely important to us to be respectful to each other and to ourselves as we navigated our individual way through this new situation.

Ten weeks! Imagine all the things you can talk about in that time! All the things you can discover about another person!

We got to know each other on so many levels. From an every-day, surface level. The "What's your favourite colour?", "What do you like to cook?", "How do you take your coffee?" level. The level that everyone sees and knows and shares easily.

We moved quickly from there to a much deeper spiritual level. The one where your beliefs, your inner workings, the "why's" of your life and the things that move you live.

Our souls recognised each other. Our flames not only recognised, but also understood and validated the other. We listened and heard and knew the other's stories. It felt familiar. His story was my story.

We had been living the same life. The same life, but with the wrong partner, both of us trying to stay true to ourselves by giving it our all until we just couldn't fight against the truth anymore. The truth that we both had so much more to give as well as deserving that same intensity reciprocated.

Neither of us knowing we had our twin flame out there feeling that same lack of love, that same lack of passion, that same desire to reach new, higher levels of connection.

Once our flames were reunited, they grew quickly. Having lived in a place of longing for so long, they knew exactly what they wanted. No more dulling themselves down, no more hiding in the shadows. Our flames came together, growing brighter by the second from finally finding their rightful place.

And so the ten weeks passed. We talked and talked. I contracted Covid-19 on my birthday and felt extremely unwell for the duration of my isolation. Josh spent a full eleven hours, spread over the day, talking to me, telling me stories, keeping me company so I didn't feel so alone.

We had our first 'voice' date, where we actually rang and spoke to each other, the first time either of us had heard the other's voice! It felt fun and silly and exciting and was another milestone worth celebrating!

He surprised me with flowers for Valentine's Day. Bringing tears to my eyes upon receiving the most beautiful bouquet of long-stemmed red roses, and with it came a little green velvet pouch that held within it a beautiful silver pendant, the symbol for twin flames, our symbol, for me to wear on a delicate silver chain.

We talked and talked and talked about everything that was important to us, things that had happened to us, things we were proud of and the things that scared us. I recognized myself in him in so many ways. It was familiar and new, exciting and comforting all at the same time.

He invited me to go with him to a five-day music festival upon his eventual return home. It would involve a trip to Victoria together, camping together, experiencing all this new adventure had to offer together only days after finally meeting each other in person.

For me it was an instant yes. Yes, to new things, yes to new experiences, yes to life! I can honestly say I had never felt this way about another human being before in my life. This man, this gorgeous Seafarer, with his big happy grin that had attracted me to him instantly, was very quickly becoming someone I wanted in my life permanently!

Finally, the date of his arrival was here! There I was standing in the arrivals hall. The noise of the passengers and the coffee shop and the baggage carousel surrounded me, and I waited calmly for a glimpse of my twin flame.

This man I had gotten to know deeply over the weeks, the time the universe gave us to fully be present to each other, in only the way our flames needed, was now in the past and the time for our reunion was here.

I was nervous, little butterflies taking flight within my body, but my soul felt calm. Calm because I knew that I was meeting MY person. My Joshua. My soul mate. My twin flame.

And then it happened. I saw him. I saw him through the crowd. A little glance at first as he weaved his way through the other passengers trying to find his way to me. And I knew. When I saw him walking towards me, fresh off the plane and finally home my flame recognised its twin and I ran towards him. I actually ran!

I ran towards him and he wrapped his arms around me. I felt his strong arms so new to me, but already feeling like home, wrap themselves around my body. The first contact our bodies had were of his arms moving around me, encircling my waist fully and pulling me in tight against him, my arms naturally moving around his neck and pulling him close to me.

We had a moment of our eyes finally locking onto each other. His crystal blue ones, so like the ocean he sailed on and mine a deep brown, so like the earth that held us. Our eyes connected, and saw, and knew. And then our first kiss. Our first kiss there in the baggage claim, wrapped in each other, with the crowd swirling around us all but disappearing, as we were lost and found in each other!

What happened next you might wonder? A few days later the words "I love you" were said.

I LOVE YOU.

It felt too small, too insignificant for how we truly felt. We actively looked for bigger words to use to convey our feelings. Adore. Cherish. Desire. We tested them all and used them regularly.

We made it to our music festival. A week after meeting in the baggage hall we went back to the airport and flew to Melbourne and spent five days lost in the magical world of ESOTERIC. We fell in love with the land, the theme, the culture, and most importantly each other.

That was the year of 'PHOENIX RISING'. The meaning touched us profoundly. We both felt like we had pulled ourselves through the deepest shadows of our lives and were emerging into this new beginning, stronger, smarter and more powerful. Both individually and together. Just like the Phoenix rising from the ashes we were reborn to a brighter, more colourful world. A world filled with love and possibilities, respect and devotion. Our flames burning that much stronger within us from being together.

I water you, you water me; together we grow.

— Brendon Nembhard

Growing into the very best version of ourselves.

We spent that year, our year of saying YES, having the adventures our flames had been longing for. We crammed more into our time together than either of us had thought possible. We held each other through the dark nights. We celebrated every milestone, every new level we reached. We continued to talk and delve deeper into our spiritual sides. We held each other in safe spaces and slowly we undid the emotional scarring of our pasts.

We both moved, one step at a time, into our awakening becoming fully supported and acknowledged by the other, our pasts falling away, and our future shining brighter than it had for either of us in a long, long time.

We made it through the wild wastelands of our previous lives and together we now looked ahead to our future. We moved in together, and slowly we have been building our home. A home where we both feel fully seen and heard and respected. A home that is filled with our love, our adventures and all that is important to us. A place neither of us – both in our forties – had ever had before.

At this year's ESOTERIC festival we survived the ESO-VERSE and all it threw at us. All the challenges and the celebrations! And there were many!! We met people whose souls we recognised, who felt like family, who felt like our tribe. And there amongst our newfound family of Esotericans, on the last night at the last sunset of the festival my Joshua got on bended knee before me. He read a speech he had lovingly written just for me and asked me to unite with him forever as Husband and Wife

"I want to show you that you are my twin flame for all eternity and that we are star dust reunited as one flame again," he said.

The sun was setting across the ESO-VERSE, the sky aflame with every hue of pink imaginable and my own twin flame was on his knee before me asking me to accept him.

There was only one answer in my heart; one answer in my soul and that was YES!

Yes to our lives together, yes to our union, yes to all the adventures yet to come our way. Yes to our flames growing ever stronger and brighter in a world that is suddenly filled with extraordinary colour and love, happiness, and a deep gratitude that the universe brought us back together exactly at the right moment, exactly when we needed each other, exactly when our souls were able to recognise each other. Consciously working together to hold sacred our divine reunion.

My soul's mate.

My Chama to his Gêmea.

Our twin flames.

Amanda Gill is a Tasmanian born author, artist and advocate. Amanda has spent most of her career travelling the world helping families in her work as a Maternity Nanny and now devotes her time to empowering women with her creative arts project, the 'We ARE Enough Art Project', with which she hopes to create real societal change for women. She is also busy writing her memoir entitled 'Pineapples' and is off having adventures with her twin flame as often as she can!

3
BLESSINGS IN A PHONE CALL

DI RIDDELL

THE GROUND TREMBLED as I strode across the paddock between the wards and nurses' quarters that afternoon in Maryborough, Queensland. My mind was in turmoil and fury after a rough day at work in theatre being scout for the day. This really means roustabout, and you better have everything that everyone needs before they even think of it. Dark and murderous thoughts flooded my mind as I mumbled to myself.

It was 1969, and at twenty-two years of age I saw myself as a young woman, a force to be reckoned with. I did not have my eye on the future, let alone soulmates. I kept my focus on the everyday, it was my survival mode. Thinking that life would go on in its imperfect, but methodical way, I was deeply unaware that my life was about to radically change. You see, life up to that time had been filled with challenges ranging from the miniscule to the monumental.

BLESSINGS IN A PHONE CALL

As my foot reached the step onto the bottom floor of the nurses' quarters the external phone rang right beside me.

'If this is some bloke looking for a date, I will give him an earful,' I grumbled. Blokes like locals, travelling salesmen, and sports teams used to ring the quarters and ask for a date. Rather like the bulk store! I was at my most officious and efficient when I took a call and told these hopefuls where to get off!!!

Thoughts flashed through my mind. Would I like a date? Would I go on a date? Not likely. How wonderful it would be to meet a loving man. Can't see that happening.

Grabbing the phone I barked in my most officious voice, '*Hello.*'

Before I could speak, a polite male voice said he was in town for a sugar technologist conference and was looking for a companion for the opening dinner that night. Would I like to go? Oh, Lordy Maudie! I opened my mouth to say no, and yes came out.

When I burst into the common room and said, 'I am going on a date tonight,' the room fell silent then erupted with everyone wanting to know why.

We immediately swung into protective action ... after all this was a blind date.

Our quarters were a two storey u-shaped Queenslander with every room opening out onto a wide verandah with slat railings, perfect for observation. That night, we did what we always did. Turned off the upstairs lights so we could sit unobserved on the floor and peer out through the railings, checking to see if we thought it was a safe bet.

If the group gave the nod, the date was on. It was our way of protecting each other. If we did not like the look of him, someone would tell him that his date had been called on duty.

As I reflect, I wore the most ghastly, hideous gold paisley shirt-dress; I thought it looked fantastic, but let's not spoil the story.

We peered through the railings as Les got out of the car. It was a nice car. He was well dressed; he was wearing a suit. That was a plus and out of the ordinary. He walked smartly and confidently up the steps, and we lost sight of him as he was directly below us. He knocked and asked politely for me.

Even in the semi-dark I could see the nods and thumbs up. Someone close whispered, 'He looks normal, he looks safe.' That was enough.

Having got the nod, away I went. That date changed the course of my life. Les treated me with courtesy and respect. He opened the car door for me and, as promised, we did go to a gala function. It was a real dinner, and I was mixing with adults and having real conversations. He did not overly impress me, but I still felt excited.

The next night he invited me to dinner, I was warming to him. He was definitely warm towards me: bringing flowers, stealing glances at every opportunity, touching my arm or back lightly and hanging on my every word. For the rest of the week, we were together at some stage every night. If I was off duty we went out for dinner, other evenings we sat in the car outside the quarters and talked. As I was working in theatre and on call some nights, I needed to stay close by. With each evening chat we grew closer.

Our evenings – all bar one – finished at 10 pm because that was curfew time. All nurses in bed at 10 pm, lights out 10.30, and our rooms were checked by the night sister to ensure we were where we were supposed to be. Once a week we could have a pass till midnight, and once a month a ball pass till 2 am.

By the end of that week, we knew there was a future for us. On his last night in town we were sitting outside the quarters when he said, 'Will you marry me? But before you answer, I have to tell you something', and I replied, '*I also have something to tell you.*'

This was going to be some conversation.

Being a gentleman, he said, 'You first.' I swallowed, my heart raced, and my palms were sweaty as I told him of my teenage pack rape, the pregnancy and forced adoption that followed. Then, thinking my life was worthless, I made a bad choice resulting in a second pregnancy and adoption. As I held my breath, tears running down my face, he hugged me close telling me it was all in the past, I was no longer that young girl.

'Your turn,' I spluttered, wondering what was coming.

'I am divorced and have four children aged eight to fourteen. They live with me,' he said. I really gulped and swallowed, yet in a heartbeat I agreed, considering it part of the package.

That night I marvelled at how our relationship had moved through friendship to love so quickly. To know he thought that I was a worthy, lovable and decent human being was a blessing.

Les dismissed the cruel labels I had been living with all my life. He saw the real me, he appreciated me and loved the *real* me.

He was the first man to show me respect.

Wouldn't it be wonderful if I could say that it was all froth and feathers from there? But then that would not be life. It took two years before we married. Suddenly, I was a twenty-four-year-old stepmother of four children aged ten to sixteen. My poor mother nearly fainted when I told her.

The wedding happened and married life became a reality. There we were living in a mill house on the edge of a cane field close to the sugar mill. Les used to jokingly say he had done a service to humanity by marrying me and taking me out of the hospital system. My officiousness and strong work ethic was so deeply entrenched, I needed to let go. As I adapted and grew into my new role, my earlier fears faded, and I gained confidence in my own ability. Les was always there to support me

Then he did the unforgivable—he took me fishing. Me, who could make going to the beach a dress up occasion was about to be tested. Les had regaled me with stories about how the kids loved going to Bakers Creek, and the whiting they caught, and the fish they had for dinner.

His first mistake was taking me there at low tide and walking me through mud up to my calves where I lost one of my thongs. It was not my finest moment as I trudged back to the car.

'Sit under the tree and read,' he said … it was a sapling with four branches and three leaves over the wooden table and splintered seats, and the ants were having a Convention.

It was quiet driving home that day.

Blended families were not common in the early 1970s. Mistake number one for me: I mistakenly thought if I could run a hospital ward, then taking care of four children would be a breeze. It could be best summed up as offering many opportunities for my self-growth.

Regardless we had wonderful, fabulous times and challenging times. We survived, thrived and our love continued to grow. The next year we had a son together, Peter, that made five children in the house.

My cooking skills were sketchy and limited because they were not needed in nursing. Now the family expected meals and smokos, and it was my job to do it.

Les loved me even when I tried to make hot cross buns one Easter. They were a dismal failure, hard as rocks. I threw them into a cane field behind the house smugly thinking he would never know, and the darn dog brought one home. And Les laughed and he laughed, and he laughed.

We were married in March of 1971, and the crushing began in June and ran through to December. I found Les had a second love, the sugar mill, and during the crushing it won every round. We never went anywhere where we could not be back home in twenty minutes, even if we went out for dinner,

Those little mill towns were a hotbed of intrigue and I was the hot topic for a long time. There I was: tall, slim, long hair halfway down my back, wearing miniskirts. I did not fit the profile of a conservative industry wife.

We lived opposite the shop; every morning the locals would sit on stools outside looking very scruffy to me, puffing away on their smokes, wearing rubber thongs and dirty feet. If I really, really needed something I would cross the road, there would be silence and all those eyes would watch me. As soon as I crossed the road home the conversation would begin again.

It was a difficult time, I often felt lost and alone. If the children did anything wrong, it was my fault because I was not their mother. Les was supportive, but he could not be with me all the time. My hard-earned confidence plummeted.

I was so eager to fit into his industry life that I let his identity define me.

I loved having a full life to lead. Only I could do everything right and I set out to prove it. It was full speed ahead, day and night.

Really, I was hyperactive; it was like I could not waste a minute. If I woke during the night my brain would be instantly alert. While I was up I would 'just' empty or unload the dishwasher, 'just' put a load of washing on or 'just' hang it out. I would wake up and cook, clean and do other tasks, except vacuuming because Les would make me go back to bed if the noise woke him, so I could only tackle quiet tasks.

If that wasn't enough, I shifted the furniture around every week. When Les got tired of helping me, even he had his limits of patience, I moved the furniture myself. It took longer because I had to empty what I was shifting to move it, but it made me happy.

Then I decided I needed a challenge, so we bought a hairdressing salon. Nursing or hairdressing had been my dreams as a youngster. What was I thinking? I had no business skills, I was going to work under a qualified hairdresser and be apprenticed to Les. It was never going to work. I had a great two years and loved being the model to try anything new that came out, especially colour. Les thought he had a new woman every month.

The bonus in selling the salon was that the profit financed our first international trip around the East including Singapore, Hong Kong, Japan, and Taiwan.

What comes to mind was our dinner in traditional dress in Japan, I went down on bended knee and kissed his hand. 'Make the most of it ... it won't happen again,' I said, and off we went.

Our family grew up, the children gradually leaving home establishing their own families and along came the grandchildren. I was thirty-five and it took a little to get used to, and Les would 'grandmaaaa' me at every opportunity.

He had a whacky sense of humour and a keen interest in music of all genres, endearing him to the grandchildren, and they loved to see the lively interaction between us.

There was never a moment that I doubted his love and support. I knew he had my back at any and every turn. When things got tough, I would say, 'I'm not feeling my best today, can you remind me of who I am?' And he would.

Every afternoon he would burst into the house saying, 'Where is my woman?' We would sit and have a drink and chat about the day.

Then he said words that struck terror into my heart, 'Let's buy a boat!' He dragged me kicking and screaming to see a seventeen-foot half-cabin cruiser that was on a trailer. My first thought was why such a big boat?

Have you any idea how much a boat shrinks when you put it in the ocean? Yes, he won that round, we had a boat and Les was in seventh heaven.

We had many magical weekends away. Our favourite was St Bees, the island was seventeen miles out to sea. It was exciting leaving the harbour as dawn was breaking and trawling for mackerel on the way. It took about forty-five minutes.

The plan was to arrive on high tide Saturday lunchtime, secure the boat to a tree, and leave Sunday around high tide; that would get us back to Mackay mid-afternoon. There was amazing fishing, shells on the beach and oyster rocks. Picking them was my delight ... eating them was Les' delight, he knew he would get the lot.

His words, 'Don't touch the bait when you have suntan lotion on your hands,' gave me a top idea. I would lotion up, then say, 'Oh, my line needs baiting.' He knew what I was up to, but always did it with grace anyway.

Lying on the beach at night under the stars, listening to the water lapping the sand was pure bliss. It felt like we were on another planet.

The bliss turned to bust one weekend. That fateful Sunday 21 February 1981. We packed up hoping to get away early. We shoved away at the boat until finally it slipped into the water, and I slipped in the sand and cracked my shoulder.

The boat was ready, Peter sitting in his place, Les started the motor, the engine started throbbing, up with the anchor, into the hold and I got busy ensuring everything was secure.

I sort of heard Les say, 'I have chest pain,' but still smarting from the lack of concern when I slipped, nasty awful thoughts like *'Serves him right, my shoulder is sore,'* flashed through my mind as I continued fussing.

Suddenly his words penetrated my mind and I flew across the boat to him.

He was pale, sweating, grey, with central chest pain travelling down his left arm, breathless and his pulse rate so fast it was uncountable. As a registered nurse, I knew what was happening.

Until now my role was to sit and look pretty and enjoy myself. Today, it was going to be up to me to get us home. This was before mobile phones; no radio, just us.

'What if I mess up, what if he does not make it, what if I collect a sailboat in the harbour, what if, what if, what if?' Suddenly my mind cleared, my inner voice screamed, *'Stop it—just do it!'*

Flying across the water, I periodically reached over to try his pulse. It was still uncountable, the pain persisting. I prayed, *'Hold on, we will be there soon. Lord, help me.'*

As we neared the harbour, sailboats were everywhere, and I was squealing, *'What do I do?'* Miraculously they got out of my way.

Up on the beach I went, the boat stopped with a thud. Someone ran towards us and it was someone we knew. Grabbing the keys from me, he raced off and unhooked the trailer and brought the car as close as possible. Somehow, we got Les in.

Stopping at the phone box, I called our GP who said, 'Meet me at the Mater, be quick'. Needing no encouragement, I took off. Les' pulse was getting weaker, it was thready and still uncountable. His chest pain was still severe, and he was getting disoriented.

Disregarding all signs and speed limits, I took off covering the five kilometres in record time. The stretcher was waiting, and he was rushed into ICU immediately and hooked up to a monitor.

His pulse was 290 and his BP 40/zero.

My heart sank as I was ushered outside.

Along came one of the nuns telling me I was inappropriately dressed in a bikini and sheer top—hell, I don't wear stockings, heels and my best dress camping!

At that moment the ICU doors opened, the doctor came out smiling saying, 'He is OK, we used the paddles and shocked his heart back into normal rhythm.' Relief flooded through me, the shakes settled, my terrifying thoughts faded.

'Can I see him?' I asked, and without waiting for an answer rushed in to see Les resting quietly, smiling as he reached for my hand murmuring, 'My woman.'

'Thank you, Lord, for sparing him,' I whispered.

That was the start of a twenty-year journey with every heart condition known to man. Always together we made it through each crisis amid the bursts of joy and sorrow over many awful, horrible times; I found solace in the unwavering love and support of Les. Together we navigated the complexities, and the unpredictable moments.

We knew that amidst it all, our love would remain a steadfast anchor in the face of life's ever-unfolding mysteries.

We had amazing times, travelled extensively, had amazing

dinner parties and barbecues, fancy dinners at Conferences, delightful special dinners at home, spent many evenings at cabarets and balls. Being named Matron of the Ball at thirty-five sent Les in peals of laughter. Life was crazy and amazing.

The time came when he could no longer get travel insurance. Not long after that, out of the blue, he was diagnosed with lung cancer and passed away three months later.

Les adored me to the very end, his woman, our special thirty-one years together.

I remember, there I was sitting with friends in the dappled sunlight on the verandah of a hospital room. It was 4 September 2002. The conversation flittered from subject to subject. We all knew why we were there. The warm and fuzzy I was getting from their presence was shattered by an earth-shattering scream of, 'Dianne, come quick'.

Three paces took me to my husband's bedside and three minutes later he was gone. Three things hit me—I was alone, I was scared, and I did not want to accept it. The love of my life, the man who showed me unconditional love, and the man who had adored me for thirty-one years lay lifeless before me.

Suddenly life as I knew it was gone.

Little did I know that this was to be a pivotal experience that would lead to a changed outlook on my life. That it would help me to release the shackles of my past and allow me to make a difference in the lives of many women.

How I would love to say, I picked up, pushed on and positively shone. No, no, no! It was, however, time; time for me to be catapulted into the life of a widow. How that term grated on me as I groped and clawed my way forward. Today, looking back I scarcely recognise that woman.

Years passed, I healed, wrote, self-published, started speaking and coaching. I could not change the past. I could change and become a better version of myself. Thanks Les, for loving all of me.

Then life changed, the time came; it was not a phone call from 1969, but an internet date in 2014. An updated blind date you might say, and I was off to meet him for coffee. That day turned out to be a great day. The details, however, are a story for another day.

Coffee brought us together, coffee keeps us together, and of course the fun and wonder of creating new memories in a new wonderful relationship is a blessing.

Reflecting back, I smile as I remember that love was just a word until Les came along and gave it meaning. He was my soulmate, my spiritual change agent. He stood by as I matured and navigated life. He reminded me of my greatness, pushed my buttons to inspire me to heal; and supported me in my staying true to the voice of my soul.

I love who I was on every part of my journey through the incredible strength found in embracing the unknown ... and taking that phone call back in 1969.

Di Riddell is passionate about Confidence for mature women: they have lived, lost, laughed, cried and moved mountains. Yet sometimes life and time get in the way. Di shares about those times ... Her gift is her ability to simply and graciously help women when they say ... 'It's time ... it's time for me,' ... to guide them as they enhance their confidence, spirit and authenticity in their world because their voice matters.

Di Riddell is the Author of 'Speak Out', a Speaker, and Confidence Coach.

https://diriddell.com/

4

I KNOW YOU KNOW

NIKI EDEN SCHLUTER

SOUL MATES

I LISTEN to you snoring next to me and wonder when I stopped finding you attractive. I am sitting on the tired old sofa in our scruffy sunroom, drinking red wine.

I sneak a glance at my husband by my side, "Mr Twit"

comes to mind. He has a thick, hairy beard and long hair. He looks like "Mr-Twit-on-speed", wow, when did he get so hairy and me so angry? I swear he grows his hair and beard on purpose because he knows I hate it with a passion. I should stop mentioning it, pretend I don't care at all.

I lift my head to look again and try to conjure up an image of you before ... I liked it when you had stubble and started to mature, 'George Cloonyish.' I smile as I recall the past, we'd had some fun.

I'm annoyed again and grip my hands together. I had such high hopes for our future, growing old together after thirty years of marriage. Planning our time, with grandchildren, in retirement. Now look at us, I sigh so deeply that I shudder. Reaching for my glass, I gulp the contents down much faster than usual, as if drinking the thick syrupy liquid will make it easier to stomach my reality. A failing marriage with no vision ... too sad.

We are about as far from soul mates as is possible. The wine helps alleviate my pain, every evening. Some nights one bottle isn't enough to dull the feelings of despair. We both know the truth but cannot find a solution.

I feel so lonely.

I look around the huge room I spend every evening in. It used to feel so glamorous when we first moved in here, our grand period property, nearly a hundred years old. It is a solid red brick house with tall chimneys and leaded windows, handsome from the outside. Inside are original oak floors and wooden panelling. I had loved decorating the polished mantelpieces for Christmas: twinkling lights, glittery ornamental fruit, and fresh foliage gathered from the mature garden made them look so romantic. It had felt so aspirational and grown up sitting in our sunroom. We'd both raise a glass of our favourite red in front of the roaring, crackling log fire on those December nights.

Now, I spend every night in the same space, but it's lost its ambience. It feels dull and monotonous night after night, lying on the beat-up old sofa handed down from my relative. The sofa was losing its oomph and needed reupholstering, but it fitted perfectly in the bay window and was wonderfully comfortable, so I had it anyway. You didn't care either way, if we were not wasting money, you were happy.

We used to save up for things for the house and garden. We were able to afford a beautiful wooden patio set for our first summer here. We treated the children to a full-size trampoline too. I smile as I have wistfully reminisced about happier times; we all had so much fun bouncing about on the trampoline.

That's you all over now though, not one to spend money on anything. This has become the elephant in the room in our marriage, almost as difficult to mention as the times I notice you looking at much younger women or the pornography I found on the laptop. It has become too much for me to bear. How did I miss such glaring red flags?

You kicked me on our honeymoon. I hid in the bathroom of the beautiful apartment in the Caribbean, too scared to come out. I made an excuse for you then and have continued to do so until now. Maybe it has something to do with my own childhood experiences?

Watching TV and scrolling through my phone, next to you

asleep again, I really rack my brain to remember when it all went so badly downhill, when I stopped pretending to see things through rose-tinted glasses.

I try to broach the subjects I care deeply about quite often: the state of our house, sometimes the state of our marriage, it depends how brave I'm feeling. I build up to the conversation I want to have with you about it. I practice it in my head, growing unusually quiet before the adrenaline rush makes me blurt it out. I am always met with cold, dark eyes, dark words, and heavy silence. You are too tired after work to talk about these things. I try again at the weekend. Like walking on eggshells, I choose my words very carefully as I know that the atmosphere is delicate and easy to spoil if I don't get it exactly right.

I'm afraid and barely know how and when I dare to mention the doors and windows, which are hardly "hanging on in there", I have to let myself in with a screwdriver some days as the handle has fallen off the front door.

There is a hole in the ceiling, which is leaking water onto the kitchen floor. It has been there for years despite the numerous requests from me and the family to get someone to fix it. Your standard response is to roll your eyes and say, 'That'll be too expensive, you never know what else they'll find.'

There is also a mouldy, filthy bathroom, an attic full of junk, ripe for conversion and much more I can add to the list as the years have gone by. I despair at the situation. It has been a topic of conversation for far too long, I could scream. I take a long, deep breath to loosen my tightening stomach as I mull this over.

I am suffocating under the weight of the devastating realisation of my fate.

My phone pings, it's my dog-walking friend, she's messaging me about her VE day street party. We'd spent most of the day messaging backwards and forwards, sharing photos of the Union Jack bunting and the neighbours in their party props, boozing at the trestle tables.

Her day looked a lot more fun than mine, full of laughter and singing. It had been full of expectation at my house, I'd hung the obligatory red, white, and blue balloons on the gatepost, made some tipsy tea with Pimm's in my pink vintage teapot and prepared a variety of rainbow-coloured vegetables to go on the skewers for the barbeque.

As usual, last-minute plans meant it didn't really get started until late. I'd lost my momentum by the time my family were gathered. My two younger children and I were sitting about waiting for my eldest daughter and her new partner to arrive. My husband had nipped into work again, my disappointment was noticeable as I was half-hearted in any attempt at conversation. Nobody seemed too worried as they tucked into the food and drink I had laid on.

The message from my friend said, 'Do you want to go for a walk?'

This question immediately grabbed my attention, '*A walk now, at 10 pm,*' I thought to myself. It was almost dark, but still warm outside. Feeling slightly uncomfortable about the time, but more curious than worried, I considered my response.

I felt a flutter of excitement in my chest about the strange request. Our usual walks had been as part of a great bunch of like-minded women, we'd all met by chance at the same local former pit tip, which has been transformed into woodland with various ponds. We had bonded as a group, there were thirteen dogs and seven of us in total. All a similar age with similar interests, mainly dogs.

We named ourselves 'The Wolfgang' and my new, very close friend was known as the dog whisperer. She was a natural with dogs, especially when it came to discipline and firm boundaries. I loved her style, she was so funny, especially when she spoke in her stern German accent, we threatened our mischievous dogs with her boot camp.

And now she was messaging me to go for a walk on a hot summer's night ...

I was already half out of my reclined position before I answered.

'I'd love to, if I can sneak out.'

'I'll pick you up outside.'

It is glorious speeding through the empty streets in her car. Windows down, allowing a rush of warm breeze onto my red cheeks. I love the feeling of freedom, the heavy scent of jasmine and honeysuckle in the summer evening air, heady and perfumed. I could squeal with joy, I feel sixteen.

From the minute we'd met, there was an undeniable connection. I was new to dog ownership, and she was an expert in my eyes. We clicked, I felt her approval and warmth as we became closer. Our conversations moved from dogs to family, work, holidays and then we just fell into a rhythm. It was so relaxed to chat.

We arrived at Elke's home but didn't go in immediately. She took my hand and led me through the streets in her neighbourhood, of course, we were supposed to be going for a walk. I was a little unsteady on my feet after a few glasses of wine, so I held on tightly.

It was so relaxing and fun, being whisked away from my usual routine and exploring unknown territory, I couldn't stop giggling. We talked and were quiet in turn, it was heaven.

When we reached her home, we went through the side gate into the garden. It was too dark to see anything apart from the patio where there was a wooden bench outside the kitchen door. I sat on the bench and watched her open the door to let the dogs out to greet us. It was strange seeing the dogs in their home environment; they were thrilled to see me and circled my legs. They weaved in and out of both of us with glee, their tails wagging furiously. A whirlwind of yellow and brown fur.

Elke had a twinkle in her eye as she handed me a drink of lilac coloured sloe gin and tonic in a tumbler. This was a new experience for both of us, very bohemian. It fitted the night perfectly. We sat side by side on the bench enjoying the easiness of the mood and our cold drinks. As the music played from the phone on the table, we joined in with "Que sera, sera" and swayed together. Bats were swooping overhead, and it all felt so delicious, like the first night on holiday, I didn't want it to end.

She dropped me off at midnight, my house was still. Mr Twit was snoring on the sofa with the TV blaring.

'Yes,' I whispered to myself, and fist-pumped the air, as I crept upstairs to bed. I was tingling all over after a wonderful, unexpected, flirtatious evening with my "friend".

Early the next morning, the doorbell rang. I was upstairs getting ready to walk the dog. My husband appeared in the bedroom doorway and threw my phone onto the bed.

'Your gay friend has just dropped your phone off, apparently you left it in her car last night?'

I couldn't find the words, he looked at me with disdain and turned and walked away. He didn't want an explanation.

My heart was pounding out of my chest. I felt sick and dizzy.

I picked my phone up out of the duvet and clumsily, shakily found my messages.

There it was …

'We need a sober conversation; I know you know.'

I began to shake from the inside out. *What did she mean?* I wondered to myself. I could hear the blood rushing in my ears and felt disoriented. Was it what I thought she meant? I needed to go out of the way, I ran up to the attic to be properly alone and read the message again to try to make sense of it.

'I know you know.'

It was such a small sentence with such a huge meaning.

She was right, I knew.

And so it began, our affair, secret liaisons, tête-à tête or whatever we wanted to call it. Same time, same place every morning, disguised as dog walking in the woods, only this time, just us, no more "walkie group".

Never had I spent so long wondering what to wear for our summer morning strolls. It was day after day of glorious sunshine, so shorts and T-shirts were perfect. I liked the way I felt attractive and seen. I was energised, confident and glowing in my new identity as Elke's girl crush. I was falling deeply under her spell. I admired Elke's honesty and straightforwardness. She had made it crystal clear that she wanted us to be together.

Each morning, she sped along my road in her grey estate car to pick me up. Her dogs were in the hatchback looking as though they were laughing, full of anticipation of the adventure to come. My two dogs bounced into the back eagerly and I climbed in the front beside Elke. We set off, music playing, ready to enjoy our little piece of paradise for a couple of hours.

This morning, she played me a song, "Beneath Your Beautiful", I felt my temperature rise and my face become hot. She looked straight into my eyes as it sang to my heart. I blushed and felt overwhelmed with tenderness. I couldn't remember ever having a song played to me in this way. She held my gaze, and I opened the window to get some air.

'How could this be happening to me?' I thought to myself, trying to make sense of the situation. *'I am a married woman with a grandchild on the way, but this feels so right.'*

The woods were covered in wild garlic at this time of the year, a carpet of tall white flowers with long thin green leaves sprawled and grew as far as the eye could see. The aroma was breathtaking and was intensified because of the heatwave we were experiencing. It evoked memories of walking by the Greek tavernas on holiday, as the kitchens were preparing food for long, lazy lunches.

I felt as though I was on holiday. I referred to us as a "holiday romance" and Elke's bungalow became "our holiday home". I felt young, alive, and exhilarated when we were together. The tension I usually carried around with me, left my body. I could reinvent myself here, forget the mess of my marriage and escape from reality.

Strangely, her home felt familiar, I gazed out of the kitchen window and thought I'd been there before. It was comforting and peaceful, I imagined us living there together. As I stood at the sink, watching the world go by, life felt so easy and uncomplicated.

Music became our love letters. Elke had created a playlist on her phone called, "Niki". I adored the attention she gave me. Every day and night I received new songs to listen to, some I knew, others I hadn't heard before. It was intriguing, I had intense pleasure in finding a private space to indulge myself and learn about her innermost thoughts and feelings through the words and melodies of the love songs. One song that played regularly on the radio was, "A Thousand Years". It became our tune. It described exactly how we both felt about each other. We were in love and felt as though we'd know each other for a thousand years.

The saying came to mind, "We don't meet people by accident, they're meant to cross our paths for a reason". We both felt at ease, as though we belonged together, we ticked so many of each other's boxes. We lost track of time on our walks and often found ourselves on unknown trails as we were so lost in daydreaming and exploring each other's life in every detail during our conversations. We became more affectionate each time we saw each other, holding hands, hugging, and touching, but we didn't cross any unspoken boundaries and kiss, although we were both tempted on many occasions. I couldn't fall asleep without her goodnight text, and early morning messages and photos of our love story unfolding.

I decided to tell my husband the truth about my feelings for Elke. My initial attempt at explaining the phone scenario had been accepted, but I couldn't live with the guilt of it all and because I was taking more risks, my behaviour was panicky and unpredictable. I felt out of control, and having palpitations became normal. My phone was permanently attached to my hand when we were apart but if, by any chance, I put it down or left it unlocked by mistake, I'd fly into the room with eyes wild with fear to retrieve it.

It was noticeable how paranoid I was. My grown-up girls quizzed me about it first. 'Mum, are you sure you and Elke are just friends?' They were sometimes at home when I went out with her during the week and were getting suspicious. I hated lying, so I explained the emotional connection we had and the enormous joy I felt in her company. They were all too aware of my unhappy marriage with their dad and my never-ending optimism and hopefulness for things to improve. However, they didn't approve and asked me how I would feel if this situation was reversed, and I was being cheated on. So, I had to face the inevitable and confess or end the relationship.

I was confused about the outcome I wanted from the conversation with my husband. I had prepared myself for it this Sunday morning, but it didn't stop me from pacing the floor in the dining room and staring blankly into the garden where he sat with his morning coffee on the sun lounger. I imagined his response as I told him about the affair and the possibility of him convincing me that he did want to remain together, despite extraordinarily little evidence of that currently.

Is that what I want? I am in love with Elke, but am I ready for the harsh reality that my marriage would end right here and now because of this discussion today? How do you even begin to navigate such huge life-altering circumstances? Am I ready to face the truth, to accept this is final and no amount of wishing and believing it could improve will help anymore? After all, I have ventured into an affair with a woman. This is completely unexpected for me, so I am certain that it will rock the foundation for my family too. I had run through every possible outcome in my mind and in every one, someone was hurt.

I had sounded it out with Elke, she said I should put myself first. This was impossible for me, so my husband and I gave our marriage one last chance, a month. I suggested that if we wanted to give it a final go, then that was enough time to test it. I was not convinced, and I was torn. Looking back, I realise I was terrified to take the leap into the unknown.

It was devastating telling Elke. We held each other and broke our hearts. I felt bereft. It went silent, my world crashed.

Nothing changed at home. I felt dismay and anger in equal measure. An unsettling heaviness enveloped me, and my mind recoiled from the terrible decision I had made. The month passed; I knew what I had to do. There was no denying the fear and regret I had, as I faced the end of my marriage, but there was also the opposite emotion of sheer delight and euphoria at the thought of a new life with Elke.

I left my family home of eighteen years with the clothes from my wardrobe, two dogs, and the promise of a new chapter.

'You move in with me, and I get to tell you every day, I love you,' were the most wonderful words to hear from the woman I wanted to spend the rest of my life with.

Niki Eden Schluter lives in the United Kingdom and has recently retired from working for Children and Families Services after thirty-seven years. Niki is passionate about spending time outdoors and walking her dogs. She has recently begun meditating and journaling. This has inspired her to begin her writing career and join a local writing group where she is working on her memoir and writing short stories.

Niki is also training to be a life coach and hopes to offer coaching sessions in the new year.

Her contact details are niki.edenschluter@yahoo.com

5

SURRENDERING TO GRACE

PENELOPE BINGHAM

TREMBLING. Memory issues. Shuffling gait. I described Fred's symptoms to the neurologist.

After a protracted interview, akin to the Spanish Inquisition, the neurologist ran a series of tests. Well, observations, really. Walk here. Sit there. Stand up. Smell this. Remember these words.

"What do you think it is?" he asks me. I thought we were paying him to tell us.

"Maybe ... some kind ... of dementia." The word resonates as a betrayal.

"I think it's more than that", he says. More? How can it be more?

"I think it's Lewy body dementia." His tone and face remain expressionless. "It's on the Parkinson's spectrum."

And so I was catapulted into the dementia labyrinth. Into a situation I knew nothing about and for which I had little aptitude.

Imperceptible at first, I'd not attached anything sinister to his lapses in concentration. After all, anyone can forget their PIN or a password. I steadfastly deflected any fleeting thought there may be a problem. But I became progressively responsible for planning, making decisions and organising our day-to-day activities. Had I been in denial in not recognising the shadowy beginnings of something ominous?

Conversations became increasingly garbled. Staccato fragments of disconnected thoughts. "What will happen if you overtake?" he wondered one night over dinner. Followed by, "Are you going to pay?"

On another occasion, he wondered if we would be locked up for the night, then asked where we were.

"We're at home and you're about to go to bed."

"Oh," he said, "that has nothing to do with gaol. Where did I get the idea about gaol?" I wish I knew.

His contorted brain was plunging him into a parallel universe with delusions, hallucinations and paranoia becoming regular visitors.

Intruders in the shed became a constant source of concern. *What are they doing here? I didn't give them permission to take over my shed. That's my stuff in the shed. They have no right. You must be able to see them. I should be able to rely on you for moral support, but if you're not going to help me, I'll get a court order to deal with them.*

Occasionally, he conducted 'conversations' with the intruders. Unintelligible utterances seeking to banish the trespassers.

One evening, however, he empathised with them. With gale force winds forecast overnight, I suggested he close the shed doors.

"No, I can't do that. The people in the shed mightn't like it."

"I think they'll all have gone home if it's going to be a rough night."

"No. They've dug a hole in the floor and they're living underground."

There were, also, moments of astonishing lucidity when his insightful observations triggered a torrent of emotions. Reaching out to me from his darkness, one day, he said, "I'm beyond help. I can't even have a conversation anymore. The words are all jumbled."

The constriction in my throat strangled any words of comfort. I was powerless to alleviate his suffering. I held him in my arms and buried my head on his chest, my tears soaking his shirt. If only those tears could wash away his confusion and fear.

Nocturnal intrusions, with the house invaded by snakes, stalking tigers, kangaroos climbing the walls and deer running amok, became a regular event. An uninterrupted night's sleep faded to a distant fantasy.

"Wake up. Wake up!" The urgency in his voice penetrates my consciousness.

"What's wrong?" I mumble.

"Get up. I've locked someone in the fridge."

"There's no one in the fridge," I mutter, snuggling deeper into the doona.

"Yes, there is." His agitation escalates.

Breathe. Stay calm warns the recording in my head as I struggle to subdue my life mantra of *God grant me patience, BUT I WANT IT NOW!*

It's 1 a.m. in the depth of winter, but trying to rationalise is pointless. Bracing against the chilly air, I crawl from my warm bed to investigate this latest delusional scenario.

"See, there's no one in the fridge. Now go back to bed." But I know sleep will elude me. Again.

"There are scarecrows outside the window," he says. "They're dressed in plastic and watching fireworks." Images of ethereal beings performing some ritualistic dance flash through my consciousness.

It would be amusing if it weren't so poignant.

I was the constant in his life. I needed to adapt; to don an ill-fitting cloak of serenity and to control the intonation of my voice. Saintly aspirations I was ill-equipped to master.

I missed his sharp intellect; his quirky turn of phrase; his clever one-liners, always guaranteed to make me laugh. But inch by excruciating inch, I began to step into his vulnerability and changing reality. To let go of the image of the intelligent, astute person I'd known and loved for half a century.

Then a new demon raised its head—the two-Penny phenomenon. An imposter, who looked just like me, apparently, poised to invade our fragile world. Another adaptation I needed to make.

"Whose house is this?" he asked, shuffling into the kitchen one morning. The first rays of sun filtered through the window and the aroma of fresh coffee permeated the room.

"This is our house, Fred. We're at home." I wrapped my arms around him. "Come and have coffee."

"I'm lost." His voice quavered. "I don't know where I am and I don't know who you are."

His eyes scanned the kitchen and the living area, searching for signs of familiarity.

"Do you know my wife, Penny?"

I held him more closely. "Who do you think I am?"

"I don't know. We haven't been formally introduced." My heart lurched as I forced down the sobs threatening to escape.

This other woman, it appears, was often rude to him and he wondered when 'the grumpy one' would be on duty again.

It was 3 a.m. and freezing cold. He needed a change of night clothes.

"Come into the bathroom and we'll change your pyjamas." This triggered a soliloquy about me being the Gestapo.

"Fred, it's cold. Please come and change your pyjamas." The soliloquy intensified.

"We need to go back to bed. Please come and change your pyjamas." The monologue, along with my frustration escalated.

"You're a mean bastard," he spat at me.

"I know I'm a bitch, but if you can find someone else to deal with these issues at three o'clock in the morning, please feel free."

My unexpected outburst had the desired effect long enough

for me to change his clothes, but my pleas for him to go back to bed were ignored.

"I'm speaking to you," I said, as he disappeared through the bedroom door.

"I'm not listening to you," he threw back at me from the recesses of the hallway.

By 4.15, I conceded sleep was futile and decided to get up. I found him in the study, wondering how all the books and papers he'd pulled from the shelves had made their way to the floor.

"I'm cold," he accused, as though I'd orchestrated the whole scenario.

I ushered him back to bed and he fell asleep. I retreated to the kitchen and consoled myself with coffee and entertained the fantasy 'the grumpy one' might restore order to the study next time she was on duty.

In the night's chasm of darkness, the despairing, negative thoughts I managed to subdue during the day, erupted into a cacophony of machine gun fire ricocheting in my head. *What does the future hold? I feel like collateral damage. Where will I find the strength to continue?*

The strength, I realised, lay within me. Until dementia infiltrated our lives, I'd never had a crisis to deal with. It was up to me to create moments of joy.

Phantom memories waltzed me to the forest where our story began. Fifty-six years. Had it really been so long? My thoughts meandered along the now-overgrown trails, revisiting the site of his family home, the house where I'd boarded as a newly graduated teacher, and the tiny two-teacher school, where my future life was mapped out.

It was here our first inauspicious meeting took place. I was nineteen. He was twenty. Tall, enigmatic with dark wavy hair and mesmerising blue eyes.

I drifted up the hill to the site of the old hall, the scene of regular Saturday night dances. Melodies from the big band era filtered through my consciousness and my feet moved in time.

He moved with a grace and agility which belied his desire to not draw attention to himself. We quickly became frequent dance partners. Love blossomed, as we floated in a graceful modern waltz or Pride of Erin or rollicked to a more energetic gypsy tap and I knew I was the envy of the other single girls.

But could the dance last a lifetime?

Lost in the rapture of the halcyon days of our youth, the negative stranger, who had invaded my being, dissolved into an indistinct shadow. A formless spectre hovering on the fringe of reality.

We rediscovered joy in the pages of photo albums. Each page the custodian of cherished moments. His eyes sparkled as we recalled stories of time spent with our beautiful grandchildren. We laughed at him tobogganing down snow-covered slopes with ten-year-old Damian and exploring the cultural fascinations of Fiji with him the following year. We were amused at him concertina-ing himself into a child's chair to share a tea party with three-year-old Josie; patiently allowing Emma to paint his toenails or sharing a building project with Charlie, who sadly has no recollection of him before he was ravaged by dementia. The person in the photos playing poolside, panning for gold and kayaking with his siblings, is not the grandfather Charlie remembers.

We also created new adventures.

"I'd like to take a hot air balloon flight and a helicopter ride," he said one day.

"We'll do that, Honey." I would do everything in my power to make his wishes a reality.

We arranged the helicopter ride over the unique beehive shaped towers that form the Bungle Bungle ranges, as we toured the Kimberley. The tiny craft we were ushered into resembled a child's toy rather than something anyone would actually fly in. Doors, it seemed, were an optional extra. The experience, however, was exhilarating. Orange and black layers of gigantic domes and spectacular gorges spread beneath us like an enormous canvas of Indigenous art.

That was astonishing," he said to the pilot, as he prised his fingers from his white-knuckle grip on the handrail.

The hot air balloon flight was a gentler experience. On a glorious spring morning, later that year, we drifted across the Yarra Valley, drinking in the serenity of the landscape, caressed by the sun's first rays. Nature's masterpiece unfolded below us with mountains, undulating green fields and the meandering path of the Yarra River colouring our world with joy.

Our Horizontal Falls adventure, by contrast, was an adrenalin-surging spectacle of epic proportions. Accessible only by boat or air, we arrived by seaplane. The view from the air unfolded intricate patterns of sand and shells resembling a vast abstract painting. A row of tiny islands appeared as a delicate necklace displayed on a bed of iridescent turquoise silk.

On arrival, we were transferred to a jet boat. With his sun-bleached hair, golden tan and piercing blue eyes, the young skipper looked as though he belonged on the set of Baywatch. The thought didn't instil confidence in me.

The four 350 horsepower engines roared to life and we skimmed across the ocean surface. The tranquillity of the sapphire water gave way to spinning whirlpools, frenzied eruptions and turbulent white waves as we approached the gorge. My heart raced as the young Baywatch skipper steered us through the narrow gap. A million sparkling diamonds cascaded around us as the spray, rising metres into the air, caught the sunlight. With engines throbbing, the jetboat rested on the still waters on the other side of the gorge, allowing the adrenalin to settle before roaring to life again and plunging back through the gap as we returned to the mother boat.

This had been the most electrifying experience of our lives. The smell of the ocean, the wind in our hair, the salt spray on our faces. This was freedom triumphing over dementia, temporarily.

Joy manifested in simpler pleasures, also. Family picnics on the banks of the Murray River. Weekly visits to the local pool. Water had always been a balm for him. Lunch in a local café.

Playing Connect 4 with the grandchildren—a constant source of delight. A glass of wine on the patio in the fading light of day.

As he withdrew further into a communication twilight, touch became our mode of communication. Therapeutic touch is the language of love. A language I needed to learn to speak more eloquently.

I stroked his face as I'd done with the children when they were small, and massaged his feet to calm him when agitation prompted constant pacing in search of some elusive object or destination.

I clasped his hands in mine to reassure him of my presence. Hands etched with the story of his life. Hands that had carried our children, mended broken toys, built us three houses, created garden retreats, stripped down and rebuilt car motors. Hands no longer rough and calloused squeezed mine to tell me he understood; that he knew I was there and he felt safe. Precious moments that sang to my soul.

The Manchurian pear tree outside the window of the room at the care facility marked the passing of the seasons. Her lush green canopy protecting the window from the summer heat and harsh light, while offering a haven for galahs and noisy parrots. Together we watched the antics of the parrots and it was always a joy to see his face light up.

The subtle change in colour was barely perceptible at first. As the days shortened and the nights became cooler, nature's palette transformed from luxuriant verdant to a cacophony of gold and rich red and deep brown.

Gradually, the tree shed her leaves to create a mottled carpet. He was always amused to see the small children scrunching through the leaves and delighted by their laughter as the leaves crackled beneath their feet.

The tree's stark, bare limbs allowed the sun to filter light and warmth into the room. We watched the clouds cavorting in the sky, sometimes softening the light or, alternatively, warning a storm was imminent.

Tiny buds appeared, poised to explode into a proliferation of white, fluffy popcorn, heralding the onset of spring. But we no longer rejoiced in their transformation.

We have returned to the forest where our story began. Released from the shackles of dementia, your spirit can run free once more.

A zephyr whispers familiar refrains and my gaze drifts to the location of the old hall. I imagine a faint smell of sawdust and kerosene wafting from the dancefloor.

I sit awhile with you and ponder this final chapter in our

journey; an experience so exquisitely painful, in which I found peace, grace and the gift of unconditional love.

Penny Bingham is writing a memoir chronicling her seven years as carer for her husband, who lived with dementia.

The book's title, *A Gift of Grace,* hints at how love flourished in an experience so exquisitely painful. How dementia's profound lessons in patience and tolerance, transcended despair to embrace grace and peace.

Contact: pbingham@westnet.com.au

6

A DYSFUNCTIONAL LOVE STORY THAT JUST WORKS

RITA-MARIE LENTON

SOUL MATES

HAVE you ever met someone for the first time and just knew they were 'the one'?

This is what happened to me, it was my first night working at the Jolly Collier Hotel in Dysart, Queensland in June of 1978, just three weeks from my twentieth birthday. When out of nowhere this cheeky bloke in a light brown checked shirt with the sleeves cut out, and stubby shorts, and work boots popped up in front of me. I can still see him in my mind's eye today covered in dirt and grime from a hard day's work, with a smudge of dirt on the tip of his nose, and his long hair covered in dust from the construction site he was working on. His first words were, "Hi, my name is Dave, what's yours?"

My smart-assed answer was, "That is for me to know and you to find out."

In that moment a flash of light went off in my mind and a voice said, '*He is the man you will marry.*'

All I could think of was "Hell No! What the bloody hell?"

The reason for my reaction and disbelief was that I had just left a relationship after living with someone for three years. I was starting over and needed work to support myself and my son. The manager of the hotel had seen me in the main street in the first week after I left John. We stopped to chat, as you do in a small town, when he said, "I hear you are looking for work, come down Friday night, I will give you a start."

Friday in a mining town pub is busy, especially in the evening when the workers have finished for the day. It had been over five years since I had poured beer behind the bar, and to say I was wasting the beer down the drain would have been an understatement.

I had the blokes helping me pour the beer when the head barmaid wasn't looking. So, when Dave appeared I wasn't expecting my intuition to kick in.

I was not looking for a relationship. So, I shoved the thought to the back of my mind. A little later, the head barmaid decided it would safer and more profitable if I went out to clear the tables and bring back the empties. As I came upon the table where Dave was sitting, he asked me, "What are you doing for the rest of my life?"

I replied, "I will be avoiding you." As I turned away I heard him tell his friends at the table, "I am going to take her out."

To which they all laughed and said, "No way! In this bloody town they are either married or going out with someone."

As the night wore on things got really busy, I started to pour the beer like a professional, so the boss decided I was good enough to be given a full-time job. As for Dave, I had put him out of my mind as I had a lot of other things to consider.

A week passed before I saw him again; he and his mates had come in, and this time they were all washed and dressed up nicely, to play a game of darts. I hardly saw Dave as he stayed in the darts room with his mates. As the time was getting close to closing time, I had to let them know it was last drinks. When they started to give me a hard time about closing time I said to them, "Give it up, I am tired, and I have a little boy to get home to."

As I was leaving the room Dave said in the softest voice, "I will be your little boy if you let me."

It was in the next week he finally wore me down by offering to take me home after work. Then the love affair started, and I finally gave into my fate. Yes, Spirit was still speaking to me to let me know he was the one. Over the next three months we had our ups and downs while I dealt with an ex who started stalking me, the construction workers going on strike, and Dave leaving to go back to Cairns.

Dave had finally confided in me he had a girlfriend back in Cairns. He said he had to make up his mind and needed time to get his head straight. His mother was to tell me later that he told her at breakfast when he arrived home that he had met a girl in Dysart, that she had a son, and he planned to make her his wife.

When Dave left I really didn't think he would be back. My ex had ramped up his stalking and was trying to get me back. I wasn't sleeping very well and I was totally frightened for my life. It had been ten long days when Dave's boss ran into me downtown and asked if I had heard from him. When I replied, "No, I don't think he will be back," he said, "Hang in there, kid, I have just sent a telegram to tell him to get himself back here for work.

It was after work on the Friday night, I came home and sat out on the porch at my mother's house when a peaceful feeling settled over me. I got up and went to bed and fell into a deep sleep for the first time in twelve days. Then early the next morning my mum came into my room and gently woke me up.

She said, "I am not sure, but I think you have a lovely surprise waiting for you outside."

I went to the front door, and parked in our driveway was Dave's yellow panel-van. I ran down the steps and opened the car door, he was sound asleep in the back, so I just sat there looking at him. When he woke up a few minutes later he said, "God I have missed you."

We had been going out for five months now and it was my mother's birthday, on 5 November. We were organising a party for her when my little sister needed to be taken to seek medical attention for a cyst that had blown up on her ear, which resulted in it being lanced. Dave took my little sister and my mum to see the doctor while I continued getting set up for the party.

Later that night, Earl, the old bar manager from the hotel came to see me and to wish Mum a happy birthday. Dave got very jealous, and we started having a fight: he was being so bloody obnoxious. I had gone inside to go to the bathroom when he made it there before me and shouted that he wasn't going to tell me what he was getting me for Christmas. What the bloody hell was he on about? I told him I did not give a fig what he was getting me for Christmas and to hurry up as I needed to use the toilet.

He staggered out of the toilet and asked me, "Will you marry me?"

I replied, "Yes! Now get out of my way." As I sat on the toilet I realised what he had asked me. We still laugh about it today, as we were never sure if I said yes because I wanted to marry him or if I just needed to go to the toilet, ha ha!

After I came out from the bathroom he stood there looking at me with his puppy-dog eyes. I asked him if I had heard right, he nodded then said, "Come on, let's go and tell your mother!"

Dave, being all politically correct, asked my mother if he could have my hand in marriage. My mother was quite inebriated and answered, "Take it, I don't want it."

The following week Dave and I had a weekend away and took Michael with us. Dave sat down with Michael and said he had something to ask him. Dave then asked Michael if it was going to be okay if he married his mummy. Michael gave him a measured look and said, "Okay! But don't you dare make my mummy cry."

So began the march to the day, we chose 16 December as that was just outside the required thirty days' notice. We met with the pastor of the Uniting Church who did not want us to marry in my mother's front yard amongst the roses. I was soon to learn our wedding was the first for his new church.

We had a few trials to get through, and at one point he said to Dave and me that he didn't think we would make it. What was his reasoning, you may ask? It was mainly because we had to have pre-marriage counselling with him; it was a little too God-oriented for Dave, and he lost the plot. We finally got through that part and then came the rehearsal prior to the wedding day. Shock, horror! The priest found out I was not having anyone give me away and he would not allow Michael, my son, to walk me down the aisle. How things have changed in this day and age. As we started going through the vows I was told that I will say the words, 'I promise to love, honour and obey'.

Up to this point the priest thought I was the level-headed one. I lost it, and I told him in no uncertain terms that I would not promise to love, honour and obey *anyone*. The priest said, "But you have to."

My reply was, "No, I bloody well don't. Where in your supposed vows does *he* have to obey *me*?" I took a deep breath and said to the priest "I will promise to love, honour and cherish this man until the day I die, but never will I utter the word 'obey'."

The priest took a deep breath and said, "I suppose that will have to do." He turned to Dave and said, "Is this okay with you?" Well, once again I lost it and told both Dave and the priest that it was not up to him to decide, and I didn't need his permission. Dave, bewildered by my display of anger, said, "Of course she doesn't have to say that."

After leaving the church Dave said, "Wow, love, I did not expect that, but it must come from somewhere." When I shared with Dave that my mother's second husband used to beat her badly and with every punch to her head he told her, 'You promised to obey me'. At the age of eleven, I vowed that no man would ever hold that over me. With that, Dave put his arms around me and said, "I will never do that to you, and I am glad you told me."

It was one week before my wedding when I had a dream about my Great Aunt Alice. She was a big part of my early years. When she passed away she was bedridden and had not walked for quite some time. In my dream Dave and I were at the local swimming pool when I noticed Aunty Alice was swimming towards me. She climbed from the pool and walked towards me, and I started to notice the sounds around me: people laughing and having a great time. The sun was shining and the water was as clear as a bell. As Aunty Alice got near Dave and me she stopped and looked at us both and said, "I wish you every happiness in your new life together."

I woke up feeling calm and serene, and I told my mum about the dream at breakfast. My mum was an *intuitive* person, and the first thing she asked was, "What colour was the water?" When I replied how clear it was, my mum said that my aunt had just blessed our marriage. Mum also told me that morning to stop stressing about what the priest had said, and to know that my marriage would last.

The wedding day dawned; I had decided to drive myself to the church, and come hell or high water I was not going to be late. Everyone tried their level best to make this happen by hiding my dress. Can I just say it didn't work, and as I was driving to the church my bridesmaid asked me to slow down, saying, "For God's sake you are allowed to be late!!!"

At the church as soon as Dave saw me he grabbed me and gave me a kiss; the Priest was horrified and told us, "No, not yet, you are not married." Ha! Ha!

Michael was sitting inside with my mum and her friend when, at the top of his voice, he wanted to know when he could get something to drink.

When we got to the reception Michael went around telling everyone we got married today. He has always reminded us through the years that it wasn't just mine and Dave's anniversary, it was his also.

We headed up to Cairns to meet Dave's family and to have a honeymoon— which proved difficult as a cyclone came in just north of Cairns, causing major flooding everywhere.

The second attempt at a honeymoon was to be on Fitzroy Island for our tenth wedding anniversary. Once again, you guessed it, Cyclone Joy arrived in full force. We made it to the island only to be evacuated the very next day.

We finally got to have a wedding anniversary/honeymoon in 2008 on Hamilton Island. It was the most idyllic place to finally have a dream honeymoon, and this time we made it back home before any hint of cyclones were happening.

Since 16 December 1978, we have had many ups and downs and have gone through some really tough times together.

It was after the birth of our daughter in 1980 that Dave was finally given the green light by the government to legally adopt Michael, it was a process that was different, to say the least.

Although I was Michael's birth mother I had to adopt my own son into the marriage. Now our family unit was complete.

We have debated loudly with each other on more than one occasion, so much so that an outsider looking in would think we are constantly fighting. We take the time to consider each other's opinions and, trust me, Dave knows if I am really mad because the kitchen cupboards—especially the one with the saucepans—get a good tidy up *very loudly*. There are times when I could cheerfully choke him, and vice versa.

We have learnt that our love language is not all hearts and flowers. Dave's first attempt at bringing me flowers was a bit of a disaster: he had gone to the pub after work, in the days when we didn't have a phone or mobile phones, so he was going to be a bit late. There was a lass selling daffodils in bunches so he thought he would grab a bunch as a peace offering. His co-worker was from Denmark and he'd had a few drinks and said, "You know you can eat these." He grabbed them and bit the buds off! Poor Dave arrived home with a bunch of stems, at least the thought was there, and we often laugh about it even now.

Dave likes to build me things, such as our beautiful furniture. He also loves to cook a fancy meal, it is his way of showing me how much he appreciates me. I try to show him how much I care in many ways, by doing little things for him and helping him when I can. I also like to allow him to feel like he has made the decision himself without my prompting, ha ha!

However, over the years there is one thing that has never changed, no matter how mad we get with each other we always make sure we say goodnight. We never leave the house in the morning without a kiss and saying, 'I love you'.

Our happy place is on road trips listening to our favourite music and singing along.

As we head to our 46th wedding anniversary I like to think back to the priest and his comment that we would not last. I have a little chuckle to myself and think, *'What did he know?'*

As I operate in the world of being a wedding celebrant I like to advise my couples of the three things I find important in a good relationship.

- Always keep the lines of communication with each other open.
- Be prepared to make a commitment to one another.
- Always care for one another.

My best policy in my marriage is to never argue without some sort of resolution. What works for me is that I just agree to disagree and let it go.

Rita-Marie Lenton grew up in rural Queensland, Australia, and her own life story is one of triumph over adversity and the gift of forgiveness. She had a long a fruitful career as a Funeral Director and Manager of a Crematorium in Deception Bay and is currently a Funeral and Wedding Celebrant in her own business, SoulCrystalEarth.

Rita-Marie is also a contributing author to several books and has authored her own books, 'Creating a Fond Farewell' and 'Miss Sweetie Finds a Home', self-published to the Amazon platform. From her residence on the beautiful Redcliffe Peninsula in Queensland, she is currently working on a third book about the relationship between her high-maintenance and media-savvy rescue cat, Miss Sweetie, and her grand-dog, Diamond.

Certified through Doreen Virtue as an Angel Intuitive, when she isn't connecting with her angelic guides, Rita-Marie loves spending time with her family. She married her soul mate, Dave, forty-six years ago and they have had a journey filled with challenges and love along the way, always continuing down that Rocky Road with each other and never giving up on one another. Family is a strong connection to all they do, having two children, three grandchildren and one great-grandchild. Their family tree is growing and will forever live on.

7

RIGHT IN FRONT OF ME

ROSALYNN WALLER

SOUL MATES

SITTING HERE QUIETLY, still, being very aware and in tune with my five primary senses, hearing the morning song of the birds, I can smell the ocean from my bedroom window and watch as it is gently ebbing and flowing. I see the sun rise over Moreton Island and watch as it shares its beautiful colours, its rays stretching out into infinity, with the hope of a new day to be part of and to cherish. I raise my crystal glass to my lips and sip on my water, which tastes refreshing, the glass is glistening as it catches the sun like a jewel. I feel a strong sense of gratitude and a sense of being so blessed in my life.

As I ponder my tasks for the day, my new venture of writing a love story about my **soul mate,** the love of my life, my support, my confidante, my *friend,* my strength, I wonder how I will ever write 3500 words and where would I even start? I have never written a story before; I have written many assignments for university in the past and they were challenging enough. I feel that writing this story will be interesting to me also, as I bring forward the memories and highlight the beginnings of our meeting each other. The story will delve into some of the challenges we both faced and how we finally overcame some of the barriers to be together against all odds, and eventually getting married. This is a story about the love of my life, the one and only person in the whole world who has shown me true love, commitment, and continues to tell me every day that he loves me even after thirty-five years together.

I reminisce about my past lived experiences, as my mind skips in and out of sixty-five years of my life, which comprises many experiences and many adventures. I am trying to extract the pieces of my very interesting and full life that would make this story captivating for you to read.

So, here goes. The big day arrived, my wedding day, 4 July 1981 (American Independence Day) I was twenty-two years old. I arrived at Mum's house early in the morning, my beautiful white wedding dress was hanging up in the front room. My bouquet of red and white artificial flowers sat in a box with all the other flowers, which consisted of a corsage for Mum, three buttonholes for my fiancé, the best man, and the uncle who was giving me away (unfortunately my dad had passed away) and the two other bouquets—posies of pink and white roses—were for the bridesmaids. One bridesmaid was my youngest sister, and the other one my best friend at the time. There was also a short veil, which was delicately embroidered around the edges, and this was adorned with a lovely diamanté tiara. My brand new white strappy shoes were placed proudly by the front door, waiting to take me to the next step of my journey, the church and beyond.

The tradition goes that the bride must wear 'something old, something new, something borrowed, something blue,' so I followed that traditon. Something old was a gold necklace that my mother had given me on the day; something new, my white shoes and underwear, of course; something borrowed was the wedding dress, my sister's friend had recently been married and it just so happened to be the perfect fit; lastly, something blue was my garter.

I recall the weather was a perfect July day, the sun was shining, the sky was blue and there was a gentle breeze blowing. I got myself dressed in my wedding attire and the hairdresser made the final touches to my hair, my veil and tiara. It was time, the car turned up and Mum and my bridesmaids went off before me to the church. The church, incidentally, was a very small, old stone English church built in 1827—St Stephen and All Martyrs. This is where I was baptised as a baby and where I went to infant school, I have lots of memories of that school.

My uncle and I were ready waiting for the car to come back

to the house to take us to the church, where by now everyone would have been congregated. The scene was set, everything was now organised: the guests, the photographer, the cake, the reception room, the honeymoon venue. I could not think of anything else that had to be done except for my uncle and I to set off.

My uncle opened the front door, the sun beamed down on my beautiful dress, the crystal beads strategically placed on my dress glistened in the bright sunlight, the gentle breeze caught my veil as it danced around my face, the veil was placed forward, and I guess traditionally used to hide the blushing bride's face?

My mother's house had a lovely garden that my late father had planted and cared for over the years, it had beautiful flowers and trees that were in full bloom in July (the UK summer). I could smell the fragrances of the flowers as they were gently blowing in the breeze and releasing their perfume. The long pathway was also decorated with an array of different flowers and shrubs which complemented the whole scene. Down towards the end of the pathway where the gate was, Dad had built an archway—an arbour—and roses of pale pink and red were trained to go up and over the structure, and some would hang down. It was so beautiful to look at, and always smelt amazing.

As I looked over to the left-hand side of the fence there stood the car where, by now, the driver was stood waiting with the door open. I then focused my attention down the long garden path where I was to walk, and there HE was, my **Soul**

Mate! However, I didn't know that he was my soul mate yet, it would take several more years for us to finally be together and have an amazing life that I was supposed to have, that I was born to have, that I deserved to have.

I gazed my eyes on my *friend* standing there, I had known him and his lovely family for years. They were friends of our family, and our parents used to hang out together and have great times. I was surprised to see him there as I thought that everyone would be at the church by now. As I walked towards him he said,

"You look so beautiful." I thanked him and enquired if he was coming to the wedding.

He replied "Oh, I can't, I'm sorry I have to be somewhere right now." I asked if he would be coming to the reception in town later and gave him the details of the venue and time.

He replied, "Oh, I'm not sure. I will see how I go for time, but thank you for the invite, I hope the wedding all goes well for you, and maybe I will see you later if I can make it." He asked if he could give me hug and he gave me a gentle kiss on the cheek, as people do in Britain when greeting someone or saying goodbye. I allowed this gesture as it would have been rude not to.

I thought no more of it, as I mentioned, I had known about him—as an acquaintance—and his family, but only as Mum's and Dad's friends. I was aware that he had two younger brothers and a sister, and they lived close by in our town, that's it really. Oh, and that he was an amazing, gentle and kind character. There were no other feelings or attachment for him at this point in my life, anyway, I was about to get married to my fiancé who was waiting at the church, and I was now a little late, but that is traditional also, isn't it?

I must admit, the driver was being very patient also, as he watched this brief interaction between my *friend* and me. As I walked towards the chauffeur, I noticed that my **Soul Mate** was watching me and he kind of hovered around until I got into the car. I saw him walk away towards the town. I would not see him again for several years, 1983 to be precise. I was to migrate to Australia after the wedding to go and meet my new in-laws, my new husband's family, and leave all that I had ever known behind.

My friend and I were separated by circumstance.

The chauffeur looked at me and said, "Where to, love?" I thought that was a very silly question, given the situation.

I said rather abruptly, "To the church of St Stephen and All Martyrs."

He replied, "Are you sure? I have seen many a bride, and never one as calm as you. Are you sure you want to go to the church? I can take you for a ride around if you want to take a moment."

I replied, "Just take me to the church."

Years later, when I married my true love, my friend, my **soul mate**, this conversation would all become apparent. But at that time I was a little embarrassed, maybe the driver knew what was really going on inside my head: that I did not really want to marry my fiancé, but I had to. I felt that I had no choice, the scene was set: the cake, the flowers, the venue, the honeymoon, the airplane tickets, and all the plans for Australia. The family in Australia were waiting to meet their daughter-in-law who married their only son. How could I let all these people down after all the money and time that went into this day? My Wedding Day!

I went to Australia four months after the wedding day, on 7 November 1981, saying goodbye to all I knew. The first few years were tough. I was told I would never see my family again. I belonged to *him* now ... I got pregnant with my first child in 1983, I saved up some money and returned to England on 8 October 1983. Three months pregnant, I desperately needed to see my mum and family. I needed care, support and advice. I wanted to come home as there was severe domestic and family violence (DFV) in my life now. Torture, aggression, coercive behaviour and the rest ...

Once I arrived home, I soon caught up with my *friend* and his family; my *friend* and I talked and talked for hours, for days. He shared with me some of his feelings towards me and he asked if I would consider staying in the UK. We spoke briefly about the possibility of a deeper friendship. My *friend* was about to fly to America for a brief holiday, and after speaking with my mum about the possibility of developing a long-term relationship with my *friend*, I was advised not to do that. Mum told me that it would spoil the special friendship that we had developed. Mum said that "I had made my bed and I had to lie in it," and that I must return to my husband at once to have the child in Australia. Mum said that the child would have a *better* life, and that I would have a *better* life in Australia. I guess Mum was coming from her own frame of reference and lived experience. I returned to Australia on 18 November 1983, to my uncomfortable reality. My *friend* said that he was devastated when he returned home to the UK to find that I had gone back to Australia already.

Once again, we were separated by circumstance.

Time passed by, and in 1984, my first child was born: a beautiful little girl. There had been some contact with my *friend* over that time via postcards and the odd phone call. My husband knew him too, and they had worked together for a few years in the UK. My *friend* loved to travel; we would often get postcards from different countries around the world. My *friend* asked if he could come visit us in Australa as he had never been to this country and always wanted to go. I thought this was a great idea, somebody from home, in fact, the first person to come out from the home country.

In 1985, my daughter was around five months old now, my *friend* came and stayed a couple of weeks with us; it was nice to see him again. He saw the life I was living behind closed doors and was upset by the situation, he offered me tickets home if ever I needed to get away. He wanted to save me. He told me to call him anytime and he would send me the tickets. Over the next couple of years, I did pick up the phone a couple of times and contemplated taking him up on his offer to go home, but at that time I never followed through, it seemed impossible.

There was a farewell barbecue for my *friend* as his trip came to an end, rather quickly I thought. We had a photo taken at the neighbour's place before my *friend* returned home to the UK the next day; my neighbours had got on well with my *friend*. I was a very dedicated wife and mother, and never strayed or looked at anyone else, this was my life, my existence, my reality. As we stood side by side to get the picture, my *friend* put his arm around my waist and pulled me close to him, it was at that moment I felt the electricity surge through my body ... it was an amazing feeling that I have never had before. My heart was beating faster, I was a little embarrassed. And from that time until my *friend* left the next day, I kept discretely looking at him through different eyes, thinking of the possibility, the warmth, the caring, the love I felt coming from him ... that little conversation we had in England, although this was never revisited until years later. Before long, *my friend* was gone!

Separated once again by circumstance.

I went on to have another child, a beautiful son; this was now December 1985. When he was around fifteen months old, I decided it was time to flee again. Oh yes, there had been many occasions where the children and I had to flee to women's refuges in Australia and the UK between 1981 and 1988. So, on

4 March 1987, I was on a plane again returning home to the UK for sanctuary.

My sister and all the family supported me in my decision. I was soon drawn back to my *friend*, and the possibilities, and *he* was there. I found the services of a solicitor, and the decision was made to formally separate and get a divorce, it was finished. Over the next seven or eight months, it was inevitable that my friend and I would fall in love. I set up house, schools, friends, life was good. I knew what my destiny was meant to look like now.

However, fate had different plans and was not finished with me yet. I learned about the Hague Convention 1980; this is where Australian children who are deemed to have been abducted (removed without permission) must return to Australia. My children were not abducted, and had an official immigration stamp in their passport, but they had to return to Australia with or without me. The authorities *would* have intervened and returned them. In October 1987, with a heavy heart, I was forced to return under duress to my former life, to my sad reality, to an unsafe environment for me and the children, who had seen and experienced too much for little ones. Once again, the only love I had ever known was taken from me.

We were separated again by circumstances out of our control.

After six months of misery and several battles in Australia, the children and I were home again in the UK. It was May 1988. Everything was going to work out this time, I could feel it, I had a plan. It would be another ten months, and another stay in a women's refuge for three months, before I could finally be free from the nightmare the children and I had lived through. I can say that just about everyone who knew of us and our story to be together celebrated my return home. We stayed with another sister who was amazing and supported us the best she could.

My Decree Nisi was eventually granted, which stated the date the marriage would end, and then I anxiously waited for the Decree Absolute, which is formal recognition of the end of the marriage. I was now free to marry my love, my *friend*, my **soul mate**. It had been such a long journey of highs and lows and now it, the wedding day, was set.

This wedding was unbelievable. This time it was at a registry office in town, I did not want or need the big church wedding or the fancy dress; we wanted a private ceremony with the people who loved us and had supported us throughout the nightmare we had experienced lasting years.

My soul mate had confessed his love for me and told me the story of how he felt on my original wedding day, when he stood at the bottom of my mum's garden and watched me come out of the house on that beautiful summer day looking absolutely gorgeous. He described the pain and anguish he had felt just thinking of me marrying that other man, and how he wanted to tell me how he really felt and how he longed to be with me. He told me he had years of trauma and heartache, especially when he had visited us in Australia and saw the life I was living far away from my loved ones and people who really cared for me.

I asked him, "If you felt that way why did you not pick me up in your arms and run away with me? Why did you not save me from years of misery?"

He answered, "Would you have come with me?"

I said, "No." As the plans were already laid the ceremony had to go ahead.

Shortly after my Decree Absolute was granted in March, we announced our wedding date, with the help of my sister. The marriage appointment was set for Saturday 20 May 1989, at 10:10 am in the York Room at the registry office. The fee payable was 48 pounds.

For this wedding day, I wore a cerise coloured dress trimmed with white lace, I wore a nice white lace hat and I carried a pink and white bouquet, my five-year-old daughter and my *friend's* little sister, were the flower girls. They wore pink dresses and held pink and white posies of fresh flowers, my four-year-old son was looking very handsome in his navy blue and white outfit. My sister (a different one this time) was my maid of honour, and she did me proud; four sisters attended my wedding, this was a surprise to me. We only invited close family members and friends, and that is who attended.

Ironically, I was at Mum's house again getting ready for my wedding. My sister and I got everyone ready. I was so excited, nervous, giddy, I cannot explain the feelings in my tummy. The car took the kids and other family members to the registry office in town, now it was my turn to get in the family car this time. There was an overwhelming sense of joy and freedom. As I was transported to the wedding venue, I was almost fainting with excitement. Now I knew what the first chauffeur was talking about all those years ago when my emotions were apparently flat ... As I arrived everyone stood outside on the pavement waiting for the bride—me ... wow! It was beautiful, I felt so special, almost like a celebrity, it was a perfect sunny day, and my husband-to-be, was waiting outside for me. He looked so handsome, and so happy to see me. We walked hand-in-hand inside, it was amazing. The ceremony began, I cried tears of joy as I tried to say my vows. In fact, as I write this, I feel so emotional, like it was yesterday, I have tears welling up in my eyes. On that special day, that we had waited so long for, there was not a dry eye in the building, everyone there knew of what we had had to endure, and there was so much love in the room. It was so overwhelming. We were—and are—very happy; my children were—and are—happy, and we were blessed with another son who completed our family and brought us more joy and happiness to all of our lives.

Circumstances finally aligned and brought us together.

I finally got the 'happy ever after,' I got to marry my best *friend*, my love, my **Soul Mate!**

Rosalynn Waller is the woman behind R & R Counselling Service, and recognises that due to work or family commitments, many people are time poor and cannot always visit a counsellor between the hours of 9 am and 5 pm. R & R Counselling Service offers after-hours counselling services by appointment only, via phone, face-to-face, and electronically, and is located on the beautiful Redcliffe Peninsula.

R & R Counselling Service offers a professional, caring, courteous, and confidential service, and has over thirty-five years' experience working with various therapies to suit the client's needs.

Rosalynn's ability to build a trusting therapeutic relationship and rapport with clients and people from diverse backgrounds aids self-management and the resolution processes.

Reach out to Rosalynn at **rrcounselling@yahoo.com**

8

CHOOSING EACH OTHER EVERY DAY

TANYA FISHER

Part 1

BEFORE I START MY STORY, dear reader, I think it is fair that I tell you I do not believe in one person being my only love, my other half, my soul mate (good grief!). What I do believe is that we intentionally choose to turn towards or turn away from our partners—emotionally, behaviourally or physically. That we sometimes have to have very hard conversations that can make us feel uncomfortable, and that we need to trust that our partners are doing the very best that they can, and sometimes I have to cut them some slack because that is what they do for me. Now, I did not know that language when I first met Darrell, but somehow, I believe we both knew that if we didn't turn towards each other we were doomed—this is how we learned that and the other things.

One day, that feels a hundred years ago, at the back of an industrial estate in Newstead, I met what I believed to be a very ordinary man. I was meeting this man because the courier company I worked for had won the contract to send T-200 telephones all over Queensland. I was going to be the liaison between the phones leaving his depot and arriving at the customer's house. Yep, it really was that long ago that we met.

I had to talk to Darrell every day at the beginning as we were setting up permanent pick-up and delivery time expectations. However, we very quickly got into a routine, and it was all going well with the occasional call to check in. Then, all of a sudden, a strange phenomenon started to occur—phones were not being delivered to customers, they were going missing. Poor Darrell would have to ring me for either a Proof of Delivery (PoD) of who signed for the phone or an explanation of where the phone was in transit. Now, this was a big client to my company so I would run around getting all the information and then would call him back quick smart. However, little-by-little after I gave him the details—that I had to ring intrastate companies for, holding for thirty minutes for post offices to check their records, and then faxing him copious amounts of paper to prove the item had in fact been delivered—he started to ask me questions about other things: how I was adjusting to life in Brisbane from Sydney, suggesting nightclubs I might like based on my favourite band, Kiss, and just ever-so-politely asking me my plans for the weekend. Little by little I started to build a relationship with the Phone Man, even when people at work would make comments about the number of phones that were going missing—I was completely oblivious!

Fast forward three months ... Life in Brisbane was getting into some kind of routine for me—I had started to pronounce the names of suburbs correctly, important when you work for a courier company, but really ... Auchenflower, come on! I had moved into my own unit at Milton, around the corner from where I worked and was loving my freedom again after living with Mum for the first six months of me being in Brisbane. I had just started going out with a 'nice' young man, a property broker, that my mum really approved of finally, in fact, she had 'set us up' because as she had told me often, my usual type—long hair, wore black, listened to a lot of heavy metal (to be fair that was also me at the time)—were just not going to make anything of themselves in life (eyeroll).

So here I was, ready to celebrate my first year living in Brisbane when disaster struck. The nice young man and I were going to the State of Origin, and he got sick; I was pretty devastated as it was going to be my first Origin as a Queenslander. Then I remembered that the Phone Guy had said he liked football and would often catch local games with mates; I wondered if he'd like to go with me? So, of course, I asked Darrell and of course, he would be delighted to help me out of the situation and take the extra ticket. We arranged for him to meet me at my Milton unit, close to the ground, so he could park there, and we could walk up together.

When I opened the door, there he was dressed head to toe in full blue, thinking as a former Sydneysider I would be a Blues supporter, yet there I was integrating into my new homeland in full maroon. We went to the game, and it was fun, really fun. Oh, to hear the tale now, he'd tell you he'd never worked so hard in his life to be funny, charming and ever-so-wonderful. Somehow after the football game, which Queensland won, and he was gone, I found myself back at my unit with a date to watch his band play the following weekend. Not sure how it all happened, but still feel it was the best decision of my life!

So, in June 1993, started the courtship of Darrell and Tanya! We were really two completely opposite people: I was loud, pushy, hard drinking and rather obnoxious, he was quiet, sweet, not a drinker and really kind. It took us both a while to understand the other and, while I don't think we ever really did at the time, we knew somehow that we fitted. We were engaged in April 1994 and married on 8 October 1994 in a beautiful tent at the base of the Glasshouse Mountains. My mum, very happy with my choice of husband, walked me down the makeshift aisle to the Kiss song, *Forever*. As my mum gave me to Darrell she said very seriously, there would be no refunds, we smiled thinking she was being funny—she was not! We were then married, so we smiled and danced the night away with family and friends. In retrospect, we both had no idea what we were doing, but we thought it would all just magically be okay!

We honeymooned and started getting used to each other, our quirks, habits and worldviews— it was a big first year. I believe the quiet man from Yeerongpilly, many times wondered what the hell he'd done, and if it was too late to run away. As for me, I was just trying to be the best wife I could be but, wow, I was bad at it.

Part 2

So, we did all the right things and started hitting all the 'right' married goals. I changed jobs, ironically joining the same phone company that brought us together, and we worked hard to buy a house in the suburbs with a pool. We hosted dinner parties and were an active part of our local community. We rescued our beautiful Buster, who was seven at the time, and then the most wonderful puppy called Bela came into our lives—nothing was ever the same!

Darrell was on his way to becoming a rock god in a great local group that was really starting to make waves, and I was his number one fan! Darrell enjoyed his work and started moving into different areas of the company, and I had found the phone company that I enjoyed and felt I could achieve in. We were young, having fun, life was good.

Then, three years in at age thirty, came the conversations about children. At first, we thought this would be a great idea. We had romantic notions of a 'junior version' of us, but as we started to talk more about it, I became very wary. Darrell had a great upbringing with a mum and dad who loved and encouraged him to try new things. While they were older parents and sometimes 'out of touch', they truly loved both Darrell and his sister.

My upbringing was not so great, very vicious. My earliest memory is hiding under my mother's long kaftan skirt, her telling me not to move until the coast was clear, where, when it was safe, I could run away, probably up the mulberry tree in our backyard. I was the youngest of four children, and when my mum finally decided to leave, I was five, but my older siblings were a part of that dynamic for years. My oldest brother, about sixteen at the time, decided to stay in the area, but moved away when mum did. My other brother, nine, decided to stay with his father, and my sister, twelve, and I went with mum. It was not an easy separation. We were all literally hunted at every opportunity. He would wait in his car until he saw mum driving and would try to run her off the road or into the rails. As kids, we were terrified, but not my mum. She was determined to leave and find some kind of peace after twenty years of sheer terror. Eventually, we disappeared to Mum's hometown, a place where she could rebuild and heal the best she could. It was hard for her; it was hard for us—we just got on with it and kept going. I was a horrid kid. As an adult, I get it, but as a kid, I was disruptive and troublesome. I never fitted in, nor did I have friends. I found people extremely uncomfortable and could never quite get them right. I had short term friends; they'd get close and then I'd move job or just stop talking to them or think of some other way to ostracise myself from them. Meeting Darrell was amazing because he seemed to like me, and I was actually grateful to find somewhere I could kind of rest in.

So, we left it for a year, and then another, and then another. Talking about children kicked up a lot for me. However, eventually, we looked at all the pros and cons and made the decision not to have children—I really pushed the idea of freedom, keeping the lifestyle we had and not wanting to interrupt that. To this day, I believe if we had had children then, we never would have made it. I would have never coped; I did not know how to be emotionally available so I would have weaponised our interactions, and I believe Darrell would have been left out until he checked out.

We decided to give the dogs the best lives we could. This allowed us to care for Buster as he passed from cancer with the best medical care available. It also allowed us to bring a new puppy, Jesse, into our lives six months later. It was the perfect life—Darrell continued to be able to do all he wanted to do, and it allowed me to continue being okay in myself, and the dogs loved us and us them.

One day, I realised I didn't like my job, so I left it and discovered what I wanted to do. A year later, I went back to a local college and studied a Bachelor of Social Science. It was great; I learned so much about how we tick, what we do, and why we do it. However, none of it really applied to me. Rather, it was about how I did for others because I had realised what I had been created for: to do good works! I did university full-time for three years, then two months later, I was in my first counselling job—I was on my way to fixing the world one person at a time.

Fast forward ten years, we'd been married fifteen years now. Dazi was working in a music shop, gigging on the weekend, and living the dream. I was working in a very intense environment, but was succeeding because I was good at my job, my boss was very happy with my work, and my clients were making the changes they wanted to make. Although it was hard, I thought I had it all under control until I didn't ... Bela was dying, and I was terrified of losing her—it changed everything.

Part 3

As Bela grew weaker, I became more vigilant. Darrell tried to step up and support me more, but I was angry. How could this beautiful creature, my responsibility, be dying? Surely, I could figure out how to fix her; I always figured out how to fix things. I was utterly powerless, and it caused me to isolate myself. The day she died I held her for a long time. When we took her to the crematorium, I loaded her into the kiln. I had to make sure she was okay and not alone until the very last moment.

The next day, I went to work as if nothing had happened, but I was not okay. It wasn't long before I was not okay in many places, and my tendency to withdraw from people became complete isolation. Darrell would cook, feed me, and then leave me alone, unsure of what to do. Then the day came when I just seized up. I never went back to the job I once loved. I didn't even say goodbye. One day, it was decided by my doctor, supervisor, and boss that I just didn't work there anymore. Instead, after four months of hiding from the world, I started a new full-time job: rebuilding Tanya.

Oh, it was horrific. There were tears, pain, deep panic, and fear. I brought all the pieces of me that were splintered and fragmented together. I unpacked every bit of crap I owned over the next two years and slowly let go of all the parts until there was only some kind of whole person. During those years, I felt like my skin had been ripped from me and that it was slowly being put back on to cover the body of this new secure person.

During this time, Darrell was my only constant. He would drive me to therapy when I couldn't, he'd make dinner, and he would not notice if I went and had a cigarette. Slowly, as I rebuilt myself, he and my therapist taught me that I could trust him, that he would stick by me and help keep me safe, that I could stop running and breathe, that I could be safe. It took time, but I allowed him to do that for me even when I was scared. I took my hands off the wheel, and it was okay. He could steer us both home. He was there every single day, watching and supporting me to recover, letting me test out my new powers of wellness.

Throughout this time, Darrell and I started redefining our relationship. Who were we now? What did we want? How did we want to live? We talked about things we'd never discussed. I stopped trying to be the perfect wife and allowed him to see my vulnerability, while he allowed me to be fragile without fear that he couldn't keep me safe—which, of course, was never his job, but he never knew that while watching me try to be okay. There were many opportunities for us both to call time-of-death and to leave. Sometimes it amazes me he did not do that because I would sometimes think to myself that this is too much for me to handle. I had no idea how he was moving through it.

Yet, best of all, we started to intentionally allow the other person to breathe, to believe that at every single moment they were doing their best. Even when they hurt the other, it was never their intention—it was just them being human. Every day, we had to choose to be with the other person, fully and purposefully. We had to choose to soothe ourselves when the other person was heightened—we had to learn how to individually be okay, even when the other person wasn't.

As I moved to the lighter end of the tunnel, I started working again as a lecturer, then as a clinical support worker. I had a different empathy and knowledge than I did before and found my feet very slowly again. I screwed up a lot and had difficulties authentically connecting with team members, but I messily got through. I went back to school and started my Counselling Master's program. I felt I was achieving again.

I moved back into the counselling field—better and braver than ever before. I found a great job where people trusted my skills, and I worked almost autonomously except for fortnightly team meetings. I happily stayed in that job until my side hustle, private practice, became too big to contain, and I felt fully ready to launch out on my own without any safety nets! I found that I believed I was deserving of success. That I, of all people, could create and hold something of value. That people would want to be part of that experience with me simply because of who I was: passionate, loud, and odd, but amazingly insightful, working with them to make their change happen.

Through our nearly thirty years together, Darrell and I have continuously turned toward each other. Not seeking emotional attention or affection outside of our marriage, with other people or distractions. This has sometimes been a balance as we both do an array of things that we are passionate about. For Darrell, it's all about playing and selling, and for me, it's about work, clients, and ongoing learning. We have a life rule that says, 'Would I do or say this if the other person was standing next to me?' Many times, I have caught, checked, and changed myself based on that question. Always making sure I am intentional in my words and deeds toward my value-driven direction of genuine connection with Darrell.

When we were wounded by life, we turned in towards each other, not out to other people. Somehow, we always knew the answer was *in* our connection, not external from it. Even when we were young and stupid, we knew emotional safety was with the other person. Hopefully, now we are old and stupid, we have a better understanding of the importance of working towards the other person. Even when what the other one says and what they mean are very different—depending upon the state they said it in—we still intentionally choose to believe that the other person wants the best for us as we do for them ... always until one holds the other to their last breath.

Tanya Fisher is a clinical counsellor, professional supervisor, and author based in Redcliffe, Queensland. With a profound dedication to fostering genuine connections, Tanya's work is centred around creating meaningful impacts in the lives of those she works with. She is currently working on the second edition of her book, "Supervise Me – A counsellors guide to supervision", which reflects her commitment to advancing the field of counselling. Tanya is passionate about mentoring the next generation of counsellors, equipping them with the skills and insights needed to make a transformative difference in the world. When not working, Tanya enjoys spending quality time with her husband Darrell and indulging in her love for Kiss music.

9
ALWAYS BY MY SIDE
TERRI TONKIN

SOUL MATES

To love and be loved, is to feel the sun from both sides.
~ David Viscott

WHEN I MET my soul mate, it was unexpected, it was random and some say it was funny. Some people don't believe it.

Do you recall the moment you met your partner?

Was the meeting pre-arranged by family or friends? Or was it totally random and unexpected like my meeting?

On the morning of Tuesday, 17 May 1976, my father dropped me off at Defence Recruiting in Brisbane where I enlisted in the Women's Royal Australian Air Force. Oh, what an adventure I was going to have.

Along with other recruits, we spent most of the day in Brisbane, completing paperwork, taking the oath to Queen and Country, and being quite nervous about what was ahead of us. On that day, I met some beautiful people, some I still call my friends today.

Later in the day, we were bussed to Brisbane airport where we boarded a plane to Melbourne. We were a little late arriving in Melbourne, and by the time we were bussed to the RAAF Base at 1SD Tottenham, we were late for the evening meal. We dropped our suitcases in the barracks, and we were marched over to the mess hall. They had kept it open to accommodate us. It was obvious to all, we were the new recruits, as we were last in and wearing civilian clothes.

The next morning our training started. We were kitted out with uniforms, shoes and hats. We had to learn what uniform could be worn when. We had to learn the mess routines, the barracks routines, the panic routines (cleaning of your room and barracks), how to march, and defence processes/protocols/laws.

And the thing they kept repeating: there was to be NO fraternisation with the enlisted men. We all had a bit of a chuckle about that, yet it was true and enforced at times.

On our first Friday night, we were allowed off base to go shopping for essentials. We were given a list of items we needed to have, in order to pass room inspection. Some funny stories there.

We were allowed to venture off the base over the weekend, however, we had to be back in barracks each night. If we wanted to leave for the weekend, we had to apply for dispensation and provide a good reason as to why we should be allowed to.

On the first Saturday night, two new friends and I decided we wanted to venture into Melbourne, perhaps go to a club, sit and listen to music, or perhaps even to go for a coffee. I had never been to Melbourne before, yet one of the girls said they knew of a place, but weren't sure where it was. We decided to walk over to the phone box (not many of them around now) and look for an address in the White Pages (another thing of the past). Some people may not remember them but they were ever so helpful.

While we were waiting, a guy, an enlisted man, pulled up beside us in his little red Mazda. He was very patient and waited while we were looking through the phone book. He then asked if he could help. Colleen said she was trying to find the address of a place she had heard about, as we were looking to go out for the night.

He told us he was heading out to a dance club at St Kilda and if we wanted to go, he would come back to the barracks and pick us up. We looked at each other and decided, why not! There was three of us, so safety in numbers.

We went back to our barracks and dressed for a night out. We went downstairs and waited for our ride. A little nervous, a little apprehensive, and a little excited for our night out.

This enlisted man, Roger, pulled up and we got into his car and off we went. He took us to a club at Lake Albert and we danced and chatted and we all had a good night. As we were about to leave, my two friends jumped into the back seat, leaving the front passenger seat for me. Hmmmmm, what were they up to?

When we arrived back to base, they jumped out and I thought 'how rude'. They said thank you and disappeared back into the barracks. I sat and chatted with this 'enlisted man' for a time and thanked him again for the evening. It sounds a bit clichéd, however, we just clicked.

When I went upstairs, my friends met me with huge smiles on their faces and Nadia said, "So, when are you getting married?" What the ... ???? We all had a bit of a giggle about that.

For the next four weeks, I met with Roger most nights, I applied for permission to leave the base a couple of weekends, which was granted because, apparently, he was well known and liked, and considered to be an honest and reliable person. He took me home to meet his parents, and he took me on my first visit to see snow in the Victorian highlands.

It appeared to be all rosy. Remember I said we were not meant to fraternise with the enlisted men? One of my instructors was lovely and told me Roger was a good guy and he would do right by me. The other instructor took the no fraternisation rule to mean just that.

If she saw me talking to him of an evening in the canteen, the next morning the punishment for my indiscretion would arrive. I would arrive back from breakfast and my bedding would be on the floor, and I would have to remake the bed. One time, my drawers were upended on my bed, as I hadn't folded my underwear correctly. Or I would be put on shoe parade as my shoes didn't shine. Funny thing about that though, I was unable to master the art of spit polishing my shoes and Roger would help me out. He had it down to a fine art. Or I would be put on re-panic as my room was not deemed to be in correct order or my cleaning duties were not up to scratch. It was an interesting five weeks and two days.

After Melbourne, I was transferred to Wagga Wagga for trade training. Roger and I would see each other fortnightly, either I would hitch a ride down to Melbourne, or he would drive to Wagga. In August, it was his 21st birthday, and his family were putting a celebration together, in Ballarat. My brother, who was also serving, drove me down for the weekend.

On the night of the party, Roger asked me to marry him. I said, "Yes", even though we had only known each other for three months. It just felt right.

The next day, we phoned my parents. My dad said he would like to meet him, before giving his blessing. In October, we flew to Brisbane so Roger could meet my parents. My dad had a bit of a sense of humour, and asked Roger if he'd like a steak. Of course, coming off a farm, Roger said yes. I am sure Dad found the biggest steak he could, and when Roger had finished it all, Dad commented, "He'd be okay, he likes his food." The next day, they went off to the races to spend some time together. They got on like a house on fire, so it was all systems go.

I was eventually posted back to Melbourne, so we were able to be close to each other. We got married the following June, thirteen months after meeting. My friend Nadia wasn't surprised when she got the wedding Invitation. Her response was, "What took you so long?" She was right, the very first night we had met.

Even though I had met Roger's parents and family early on, and it seemed I was accepted as his girlfriend, his dad was not happy when we decided to get married. He did try a number of ways to put a spanner in the works so it wouldn't go ahead. That's another story for another time. I say it was because his dad had already picked out a wife for Roger, a farmer's daughter, and I didn't fit the agenda. I was a bit more outspoken too, which probably didn't help my cause. Anyway, we both defied the odds and proceeded with our plans.

Our wedding day was wonderful, a winter wedding in Brisbane. I arrived at the church with my dad, and we had to wait, as Mum hadn't arrived, even though she had left before us. Our friend who was driving her, had taken a wrong turn and had been momentarily lost. Good one, Peter. My dad turned to me and said, "Are you sure about all this? You can still change your mind." Nope, that was not happening. I knew this was what I wanted. My dad and Roger became the best of mates, and to this day, we all miss my dad so much.

I discharged from the RAAF in December 1979, as back then, serving women struggled to progress through the ranks if they were married. The man was given preference and married couples were rarely posted together. Upon my discharge, Roger was posted to Amberley, Queensland. This was our first posting, our first experience of a removal (and all the paperwork to go with it), our first experience of a married quarter inspection, and our first experience of travel entitlements and requirements. A steep learning curve.

We moved into a married quarter after spending some time in a motel. I scored myself a job and all was good. And then I found out I was pregnant. My new employer was not too happy, however, they did support me and kept a position for me right up until the month before the scheduled birth. Six weeks after the birth, I was back in hospital due to some complications. Roger had to not only look after me, but our baby also.

Three years later, our second child was born, and again, complications came into play. Got myself sorted, and our new son had to go into hospital at six weeks old for surgery. Again, Roger stepped up and looked after us all.

We were then posted to Darwin. I gained employment in a bank, and Roger got to do the job he loved. Whilst there, my dad suffered a heart attack and I had to fly back to Brisbane. I personally, had another medical situation requiring surgery. Roger too, had to have an operation. And to top off our stay in Darwin, I was the victim of a bank hold-up. For me, it was time to leave Darwin. I had had enough of being too far away from family.

Roger was posted to Wagga Wagga in NSW. It was here we purchased our first home. Another surgery for me. My dad had been diagnosed with cancer.

Then another posting to Newcastle. Yet another surgery for me. My brother passed away. Roger went to New Zealand on an exchange posting, and I had to pack up the kids and send them off to school not knowing if we would have a house to come back to, as bushfires were really close to the property. Before Roger returned home, we had to lay our beautiful pet to rest, as he had suffered a massive seizure. My older brother had a nasty accident. Never a dull moment.

Finally, we moved back to Brisbane, to support my mum, as Dad was in the later stages of his life, and sadly passed within three months of our return.

We purchased our second home and the family settled in. The boys started at yet another school, the eighth for the oldest and fifth for the youngest. I had been lucky enough to transfer with the bank. Roger discharged from the RAAF and found it difficult to settle into a routine and unstructured employment.

Roger served almost twenty-one years in the RAAF, and was often on shift work or deployed for periods of time, for exercises and courses, and his trip to New Zealand. It was like I was a single parent sometimes, as it was only me at home.

And yet, we all survived.

Our boys grew up, left school, and got jobs (not always close to home). I was actually one of 'those mums' who couldn't wait for the boys to leave home. Does that make me a bad mum? No, I don't think so. It meant I had done the best job I could, in teaching the boys how to live and survive and thrive in life.

The oldest has worked out at Uluru (Ayres Rock as it was then known), on fishing trawlers, the almond farms along the Murray River in Victoria, done landscaping and farm work. The younger son too, has had a variety of jobs from tyre-fitting and shop management, airport security, hotel security, NDIS worker to working at the airport. I believe because we moved so regularly, they were able to adjust to whatever opportunity came their way.

Both boys have given us grandchildren (one of the best things about being a parent), who we love and adore. We still have to put in boundaries about our role in their upbringing, as I wasn't going to be a full-time grandmother. We do help out as much as we can, if and when we are available.

Roger is fully retired now, and for all intents and purposes, so am I. I still do my writing, for myself and others as a ghostwriter, however, I am not going to go out and get a job. Well, not if I can help it. Definitely not something in my plan. We've just purchased a new vehicle and a caravan, so you can see what is in our plan. Getting out there and discovering places we haven't seen yet, at our leisure and for pleasure.

We are lucky though. We have been fortunate to have seen a lot of Australia and had the experience of travelling overseas to New Zealand, parts of Asia and the Middle East, and the United States. Still want to do more of that too.

Life has taken us on many ups and downs and adventures, through fun times and sad times and travelling. It has never been an 'easy ride' yet we have stuck together through thick and thin. I'm sure sometimes we were on slippery ground, yet we always found our way out, or through, the tough times.

I have had many medical issues requiring surgeries, and having to explain to the two boys wasn't always easy. Roger never faltered. He stepped up each and every time, to ensure I was taken care of and recovering, and the boys never missed out on their activities.

Roger says he has done well, as he has served a number of life sentences. Twenty-one years of RAAF service and the years we have been together. He tells people not only have we survived, but we also still like each other and still talk to each other.

And I think that is one of the best things that we have always done. Talked to each other. About anything and everything. Nothing was off limits.

We talk, we laugh, we respect each other's space and limits, and we acknowledge that we have our own interests and likes. Yes, we have joint interests and things we do together, yet we also go our separate ways to enjoy the things we like doing by ourselves, or with others.

We have supported each other through our health challenges. We have supported each other through our employment battles. Between us, we have lived through three redundancies. I encouraged Roger to leave one employer as I could see it was physically and mentally destroying him. Roger has supported me through many courses and studying, and setting up my own business.

Don't smother each other. No one can grow in the shade.

— Leo Buscaglia.

We have both lost our parents, so our children no longer have grandparents, and their children won't get to know their great-grandparents.

Through thick and thin, no matter what was thrown our way, we are still here, together.

When the opportunity arose to be a contributing author to this book, 'Soul Mates', Roger and I had just celebrated our forty-eighth year together, forty-seven years as husband and wife. I think that says a lot.

Earlier I said, "We just clicked." My friend Nadia had our measure the very first night we met. She knew before we did.

I'm going to confidently say, Roger and I chose well. May we have many more years together, doing life our way.

We love in another's soul whatever of ourselves we can deposit in it;
the greater the deposit, the greater the love.

— Irving Layton.

We are truly Soul Mates.

Terri is a multiple International Best-Selling Author, Ghostwriter and life coach. She has written her own books, contributed to numerous compilation books and is now writing manuscripts for others. Her preferred genres are memoir, well-being, lifestyle and personal development, with some small business added to the mix

Terri has been featured in The Corporate Escapists and

Disruptive Publishing magazines and has been interviewed on Voices on Fire; Empowered to Shine; Fast Forward Your Entrepreneur Journey; and The Corporate Escapists podcasts.

She is the face of **Connect Within**, and her clients are heard, validated, acknowledged, encouraged and supported to find the solutions they are searching for.

Terri aspires to inspire the people she meets to reach their potential, as inspiration leads to motivation, and motivation leads to action, providing results.

Her life has been a journey of ups and downs, trials and tribulations, both personally and professionally. She is a life-long learner, seeks out new opportunities, is an avid reader and loves to travel.

Go to www.connectwithin.com.au to connect with Terri.

10

WIND BENEATH MY WINGS –

TRISH SPRINGSTEEN

SOUL MATES

ON 8 FEBRUARY 1975 my life took a sudden turn, though I was not to realise this for many months.

I was eighteen years old and had been living in Melbourne for a year studying for my Associate Diploma Medical Records Administration. I had grown up, went to school and lived most of my life in Canberra. That was where all my friends were, however, I had decided on leaving high school that I wanted to be a Medical Records Administrator working in hospitals coding medical records. Alas the only place to study for this new career was in Melbourne. So, I packed my bags, left home and settled in a flat in Hawthorne, Melbourne. The flat was right near the train station, so it was an easy journey to grab the train into the city and the tram up Swanston Street to Lincoln Institute. I was not quite alone, as a cousin lived two floors above me.

My first year in Melbourne was spent focussed on my studies, travelling back and forth and getting to know Melbourne with all its four seasons in one day. I had my favourite SF and Fantasy bookstore which I walked right by in Swanston Street. I didn't make friends easily, being rather shy, and was happy to study and hibernate in my flat.

My second year started with me being a bit more adventurous. I had a flatmate and had ventured out a couple of times with a group of student doctors and nurses for drinks. In fact, not long before that pivotal day, 8 February, I had said to Mum on one of our phone calls that I had met Peter, a student doctor, and we had been out for a drink. This was pretty good for a shy introvert. This was also going to prove to be a rather funny coincidence in the not-too-distant future.

So, there I was halfway through my studies, making plans for where I was going to go when I finished at the end of the year. Canberra the familiar was calling, as was Perth. For some reason I thought it would be good to go somewhere different. I was not to know that all those plans were ultimately to go out the window!

Saturday 8 February dawned with no hint as to the changes that were to occur during the day. My flatmate had plans to go out swimming in the afternoon. She had asked me to go, however, I declined as I had a raging cold, red nose, red eyes, and was sneezing my head off. I thought an afternoon at home with my tissues and a good book was a much better place to be. I had no premonition that destiny, some may say, was rushing towards me.

Later that afternoon, there was a knock at the door. I was not expecting anyone so was surprised to open the door and there was a man at the door. He asked to speak to my flatmate (he had been told that she would be open to going out on a date). I told him she had gone out for the afternoon and could I take a message. He paused for a moment, looked at me and said, "Hang on a moment, I will be back." I'm not sure why I didn't close the door. Was there a bolt of lightning, a premonition, a sudden beat of my heart, anticipation of an unlooked-for event? No, there was just me waiting to get this over with so I could go back to my tissues and my book. Remember, I had a red nose, eyes streaming – most certainly not looking my best.

Anyway, this man came back, he had put his glasses on (this always makes me smile – I don't know why – him putting his glasses on, presumably to have a better look at this person standing in the door) and he introduced himself as Peter, Peter Springsteen. I asked him in for a coffee and we got talking.

I discovered he had just had his birthday two days ago on 6 February. Mine was coming up on 21 February. He asked me out to celebrate his birthday and my upcoming one. It was Valentine's Day the next week as well. I am not sure why I said yes, but I did. I was going on a date! We had talked for a very long time.

Our first date came, it was on a Friday a week later. There are three things that stand out for me from that date. Looking back, I can see it was a foregone conclusion, I just hadn't realised what had happened. I often say I am a slow learner and am often the last one to realise momentous events. You could say that I often walked around in a world of my own. At least that was what I was like at that point in my life.

I can't remember where we went for dinner, however, I do remember the dog we rescued and spent hours driving around looking for a RSPCA depot to drop the dog off. I do remember it was a full moon, a beautiful night and we ended up on St Kilda beach and I absolutely do remember the beautiful poetry that Peter said to me. Poetry that he had written. What can I say, he stacked the dice. A full moon, animals, beach, poetry – I was hooked only I didn't realise it.

Well, that was the start of a relationship. I was in a serious dating relationship. My last year studying in Melbourne was awesome. We went everywhere – he picked me up from class on his motorbike. He took me to excursions in his VW Beetle. I have fond memories of that small car.

When I wasn't studying, we spent time together. Not long after we met, my mum came down to Melbourne to visit, Peter was with me at the flat when she arrived so I could introduce him. Now, remember I had told mum that I had gone on a date with Peter the student doctor. Well, it was rather funny looking back, but a bit embarrassing at the time.

I introduced Peter to Mum and her first words were, "Oh, you're the student doctor, nice to meet you."

I quickly scrambled correcting the impression and advised, "No not that Peter – this is a different Peter, the telephone technician."

A few months after our first meeting, Peter said to me, "I am going to marry you."

I laughed and said, "Nope, not ready for marriage. I have things to do."

"That's okay," he said, "I knew I was going to marry you by the end of our first date. I can wait."

I put it out of my mind and concentrated on the fun we were having and on the amazement of having a serious boyfriend. Oh, and in there somewhere was studying to complete my second year. I got to meet his family: his mum and dad, elder brother and his twin. Yes, my Peter was one of twins. At that time they looked identical (the years have slowly impacted differently so now, not quite identical), but as I was to slowly discover, completely different in personality. I am happy to say, that from my perspective I ended up with the best twin.

Things progressed during that year. I was happy in my world. I had given no thought to Peter's declaration in the early months of our relationship. I had put that word marriage right out of my mind. I lived in the moment. Until the end of the year was in sight. I had had my final exams and decisions had to be made. Where was my life going to go, what direction would I head in?

So, there we were towards the end of that year in the flat. We were talking about what I was going to do, and I had said to Peter it would not be in Melbourne. I was going to go back to Canberra to work in one of the hospitals there. That was when Peter asked me to marry him. It was then I stopped and really thought about being in Canberra without him, he had snuck into every corner of my life, he was just there and to be without him was not going to work. I realised what he had started on that first date, with the full moon, the poetry, and what we had put together during the past year was what I wanted for my future. I said, "YES."

Things moved fast, Peter left his job, gathered his things and promptly moved to Canberra with me. We were engaged and were looking forward to spending a year together – yes, we decided to get married in November 1976. I wanted to spend the year working in the field I had studied, and we needed to establish ourselves in Canberra. Well, as they say the best laid plans ... In the time I had been away studying, Medical Records Administrators had become a big thing in the hospitals and now there was nowhere for me to work in Canberra. So that engagement year ended up with Peter in Canberra and me working in Sydney. The road between Canberra and Sydney became very well worn with Peter coming up most weekends to spend time with me. I can tell you an engagement year apart was not what I planned, however, I think it was a benefit because it tested our relationship and our love. If it survived that then it could survive anything. Prophetic words – not knowing what the future eventually brought to us.

We were married on 27 November 1976. Peter says he remembers because of *Seventy-Six Trombones* (a line from the song, "Seventy-Six Trombones led the big parade ..."). I was twenty and Peter was twenty-eight – yes, he is eight years older than me. I turned twenty-one in February 1977, I didn't have a twenty-first birthday party because of the wedding being so close. It was a big wedding, and yes it would be no surprise to anyone knowing me that the colour scheme was Purple. A very

70s wedding: the guys in grey suits with big lapels, my wedding dress was medieval, Ann Boleyn-ish themed – long draping sleeves.

In November this year, 2024, we will have been married forty-eight years. We have two children: Rochelle and Craig. Have all those years been utter bliss? No, we have had our ups and downs like any marriage. We have moved several times around Canberra, then from Canberra to Bald Hills, Brisbane in 1989 and then north of Brisbane to Narangba, Caboolture, and finally in Morayfield where we are now. There has been one serious argument and three big crisis situations. I have worked in three different careers and I started a business in 2006, which is still going today. Peter has had jobs, lost jobs, retired. We have comforted ourselves through family deaths, rejoiced with marriages (one of those marriages was one of four of my closest friends marrying Peter's twin). We are still together.

Those crisis situations were the loss of our son Craig to suicide in 2007, Peter's prostate cancer and my breast cancer. Any one of these could have caused a break in the marriage. They are all stressful situations.

We lost Craig on Monday 3 October 2007. We started that day a family of four and ended that day a family of three. Craig was gone. My darling husband who never really gets angry, was so angry when we found him. I never want to hear again the sounds of anguish from Peter that I heard that evening. The next day dawned – a new day, a life without Craig. Peter and I held each other, and we both knew that this was a situation that could break a marriage. We vowed to be there for each other, to live each day in memory of Craig, to hold him in our hearts – and we have. Our life changed, our daughter was married and living in Orange County California USA. She can't have children. Our future as grandparents was gone. We are still together.

Peter's prostate cancer and my breast cancer brought changes, some physical, some emotional. We worked through them. In truth, losing Craig was a big bar to measure any other situation against. We worked it out together. We are still together.

My business has had its ups and downs. Through it all, Peter has always been there for me, he has always supported me in anything I wanted to do. He believes I am the most brilliant speaker, coach and mentor around.

He often asks, "Why do others not realise that?"

I say to him, "Darling, they do not all see me through your eyes." He truly believes there is nothing that I can't do.

We are not the same people who sat on that beach under the full moon all these many years ago, and that is okay because we have grown together, changed together. Life has thrown things at us and we have thrown things at life. We have made memories, good and bad. We have made those memories together.

I often think, as many of us do, 'What if?' What if we had not lost Craig? What if we had not had our medical issues? What if we had not moved to Brisbane? Would that have made things different?

What if I had not stayed home that day fifty years ago and was not there to greet that man who came that day to the flat.

Would things be different? On that small decision to stay home a whole life has been built. Would things be different? Probably – would things be better? I don't know.

I do know that right here at this moment typing these words – I would not change my life, even knowing the things that have happened, I would not change that moment fifty years ago when I opened the door and the person on the other side said wait, I will be right back. He put his glasses on, came back and here we are.

Is Peter my soulmate? He is my other half, my rock, my foundation, my friend. He is the father of our children. He is the one I can yell at, who puts up with me, when I am cranky, when I am floundering. He is the one who does most of the cooking, the cleaning, so I can run my business, go out and speak, write my books. He is the one I can fight with and then go to bed at night knowing he will be there for me. He is the one I say crazy things to, and laugh with; he is the one who I listen to when he shares his conspiracy theories and who loves me even when I don't agree with him. He is the one I worry about and who worries about me. He is the one who adores my family and will do anything for them and puts up with them.

He is the one who calculates he will live to be 109 because he knows I want to reach 100 to get my telegrams and that I want him to be there with me.

He is the wind beneath my wings.

Patricia and Peter – two Ps in a pod.

If all of that is the definition of a soulmate – then I guess that is who my Peter is now and ever will be.

Trish Springsteen is an exceptional Confidence Coach and Get Known Be Seen Specialist, renowned as Australia's Leading Expert in Empowering Introverts. With an impressive track record as a multi-international award-winning mentor, speaker, and bestselling author, Trish has established herself as a prominent figure in the industry. As the host of Get Known Be Seen WebTV, she amplifies her impact on a global scale.

Known for her love of Purple and helping her clients to own their uniqueness, it is no surprise Trish has recently launched her Purple Unicorn® Academy where she works with you to find the gold nuggets in your business to promote and market yourself. Trish is the author, co-author, contributing author of 20 books and is featured in *The Corporate Escapists*, *Mo2vate* and *The Disruptive Author* Magazines.

When she is not mentoring, speaking and writing, Trish indulges in her love of reading SF and Fantasy, and traveling.

11

THE FINAL CHAPTER

DEBORAH FAY

SO NOW WE come to the end of the book where we say farewell. Each and every one of us who have contributed to this book sincerely hope that you have enjoyed reading our stories and that we have left a positive imprint on your heart.

Please feel free to reach out to Disruptive Publishing at www.disruptivepublishing.com.au if you would like to connect with any of our authors - we would love to hear from you.

We'd also love for you to leave a positive review when you get the chance.

And finally, we wish you the very best and hope your life is blessed with the love we all deserve.

Much love from all of us

12

BUT WAIT, THERE'S MORE...

DEBORAH FAY

HAVE you thought about becoming an author?

Stories are everywhere. They're tucked into every conversation we have, shared over meals, whispered to friends in confidence, and often replayed over and over in our minds.

Sadly though, many people think their story doesn't matter enough to be written down, let alone published.

Becoming an author often seems like something reserved only for people with monumental experiences—people who have traveled the world, overcome impossible odds, or accomplished something groundbreaking and worthy of worldwide accolades.

For most of us, life feels so much more ordinary, and the idea of putting our stories on paper feels like too big a stretch.

Something really interesting happens however when we start to share out stories. They connect us in ways that little else can.

Sometimes, sharing even the simplest truths has the potential to impact someone else's life, to offer them insight, encouragement, or a sense of belonging. In a world where so many people feel unseen, sometimes the most impactful thing you can do is simply to share your truth. It's that powerful.

Why *Your* Story Matters

I promise you that everyone, including you, has a story worth telling, and often, it's the moments we consider ordinary that resonate most with others.

Our struggles, our small victories, our moments of doubt—they are the pieces of humanity that link us together.

When I began sharing parts of my own story through publishing, it became clear to me that my experiences weren't just mine; they were reflections of a much larger human experience. My challenges and triumphs, my fears and joys, mirrored those of others who were also walking their own, unique paths.

Sharing your story as an author means giving others permission to see themselves through a different lens. When we write and we allow ourselves to be vulnerable we let others know, "You're not alone." In this way, stories can bring relief and healing to those who feel isolated in their experiences.

Each time I receive a message from someone who has connected with something I've written or something I have published for another author, I have gained a deeper understanding of the importance of putting our stories out into the world.

BUT WAIT, THERE'S MORE…

Writing to Heal and Grow

Becoming an author isn't just about sharing your story with others though; it's also about understanding it for yourself.

Writing forces you to look at your life with fresh eyes, to search for meaning in the pain you've experienced and to make peace with your past. It's liberating going through the process, and in my opinion, this is the most valuable part of writing your story.

Often, we get wrapped up in the stories we tell ourselves, sometimes without even realising we're holding onto them, and writing has a way of unraveling those old stories and revealing new, and more empowering perspectives.

When an author begins the process of writing their story, their past transforms from a collection of memories into a narrative and a journey of growth that has brought them to where they are today.

The things they once saw as failures begin to look like stepping stones, and the challenges they faced reveal themselves as necessary lessons, even if they were deeply painful to relive. And through this process, an author starts to heal from thoughts and feelings they didn't even known they had been carrying around with them everywhere they went.

Inspiring and Connecting with Others

Then there is the joy that comes when you realise that your words might spark something meaningful in someone else.

Perhaps they'll find courage in your resilience, hope in your vulnerability, or laughter in a moment you've shared. Just as we lean on the stories of others to navigate our own lives, your story can become a guidepost for someone who feels lost, a source of light for someone searching in the dark.

There's something uniquely beautiful about knowing that the pages you've written will one day be held by someone you've never met.

I've imagined readers recognising themselves in my words, laughing or tearing up as they see glimpses of their own lives reflected back at them. It's a reminder that our stories don't belong to us alone; they are part of a greater tapestry, woven together by the experiences we share.

Leaving A Legacy

Writing your story is a chance to leave behind something lasting, to give future readers a glimpse into your life, your mind, your heart.

You don't have to share every detail of your life but in sharing parts of it you can capture the essence of what you've learned, what you believe, and the moments that shaped you.

As an author, you have the privilege of shaping how others experience your story, of framing it in a way that will resonate with those who read it long after you've written it. How cool is that?

This sense of legacy can feel intimidating, but it's also deeply empowering.

I remind myself that every book I publish, every piece of writing I make accessible to readers through my work, becomes part of the collective human experience.

When we choose to share our stories, we become part of that collective, contributing our voice to the endless library of human experience. And while writing your story may have begun as a personal journey, it ultimately becomes something bigger—a gift to the world and to everyone who will read it.

The Ripple Effect of Your Story

One of the most beautiful things about stories is the way they ripple outward, reaching people in ways we can't predict.

Maybe someone will stumble upon your words at a time when they need them most. Perhaps your story will inspire someone else to share theirs, creating a cycle of storytelling that touches countless lives.

When we write, we send out echoes, knowing they may reach others long after we've set down the pen.

In becoming an author, I've personally learned that the importance of sharing your story goes beyond yourself. It's about creating connections, igniting change, and leaving behind a legacy of truth. It's about giving others permission to own their stories, too.

So, if you've ever wondered if your story matters, let me be crystal clear: ***it does***.

By embracing your experiences and offering them to others, you're contributing to something larger than yourself.

And that is the power—and the beauty—of becoming an author.

When you are ready to explore the idea of becoming a published author, reach out to me at deb@disruptivepublishing.com.au. I'd love to help you find your way.

www.ingramcontent.com/pod-product-compliance
Lightning Source LLC
Chambersburg PA
CBHW072208070526
44585CB00015B/1242